C000110407

Oliver Whitby School
Chichester

A HISTORY

Portrait of Oliver Whitby, painted by unknown artist and presented to the School by Old Scholars in 1887. Attributed to Mary Beale, and reproduced with kind permission of the Museum and Governors of Christ's Hospital.

Oliver Whitby School
Chichester
A HISTORY

compiled by
Peter J. Hughes

Phillimore

2002

Published by
PHILLIMORE & CO. LTD
Shopwyke Manor Barn, Chichester, West Sussex

ISBN 1 86077 212 9

Printed and bound in Great Britain by
THE CROMWELL PRESS
Trowbridge, Wiltshire

Contents

List of Illustrations vii

Acknowledgements viii

The Nineteenth of February 2002: A Prelude ix

List of Subscribers xii

Introduction xiii

One   Oliver Whitby: Life and Times, 1600-1702 1

Two   The Will and Foundation of the School, 1702-1712 7

Three   The Eighteenth and Nineteenth Centuries, 1712-1870 13

Four   Headmaster Ballard: The 'Drains' and Prior's Scheme, 1871-1904 .. 35

Five   Enlightenment to Decline and Fall, 1905-1949 63

Six   Times Remembered 81

Seven   Epilogue—All Was Not Lost 101

Postscript 113

Appendices

i   Trustees and Governors 115

ii   Headmasters 116

iii   Roll of Honour—Best Scholar 117

iv   Inscription on Playing Field—Memorial Stone 118

v   Bathing Instructions—Easter Term, 1939 119

vi   Letter given to Boys at the Closing of the School 120

vii   Copy of Programme of Plays performed by the Boys 121

viii   'Strength and Wisdom' by William James Barnes 122

ix   Order of Special Choral Service 123

Select Bibliography 129

Index 131

To all boys, past, present and future,
who have had, or will have, the honour to wear the Oliver Whitby badge

List of Illustrations

Frontispiece: Portrait of Oliver Whitby

	Old Boys, outside the school, 2002	xi
1.	First page of Oliver Whitby's will	6
2.	Original school building	12
3.	The wooden Blue Coat Boy	19
4.	Interior of West Wittering School	29
5.	Charles R. Ballard	35
6.	Oliver Whitby boy in 1865	36
7.	Full School/Southgate House, 1897	56
8.	Ready for cricket in the 1890s	57
9.	Oliver Whitby School, West Street, Chichester	62
10.	School Dining Hall	64
11.	Classroom, Tower Street school building	64
12.	Headmaster's desk	65
13.	School cricket team	65
14-15.	Summer scout camp	66
16.	Swimming party	67
17.	Proud 'Big Game Hunter'	67
18.	Mrs Fairbrother, Matron	67
19-20.	Mr and Mrs Spendlove	69
21.	Boys walking to the Cathedral, 1932	70
22.	Group of boys in the playground, 1933	70
23.	Boys clearing debris from bomb damage	71
24-25.	Annual Summer Camp	72
26.	Mr Spendlove with 'Colonel', *c.*1946	74
27.	Mr Spendlove, West Broyle, 1948	74
28.	1948 football team	75
29.	Reg Courtney in his Sunday best gown	76
30.	The twin Hoskins brothers	76
31.	Mrs Marsh with her son William and grandson Peter	77
32.	John (Ricky) Haffenden and Robert (Bob) Ide	77
33.	The Dean of Chichester bidding farewell to the boys, 1949	78
34.	Final photograph of the boys, headmaster and governors, 1949	79
35.	The Sick Bay, *c.*1920	83
36.	Freehand drawing of front of school	85
37.	Group of boys in front of gymnasium, 1946	86
38.	Head boy, *c.*1920s	87
39.	New boy in his Sunday best	87
40-41.	Oliver Whitby memorial and stained-glass window, Chichester Cathedral	89
42.	The oak staircase	90
43.	Boys sitting on the school garden wall	94
44.	The Dining Hall, *c.*1920s	96
45.	Old Oliver Whitbyians Association Dinner	98
46.	Two Old Boys standing beside the 'Roll of Honour—Best Scholar' board	116

Acknowledgements

The publication of this book, satisfying, as it does, a personal ambition to see the story of Oliver Whitby and his School recorded as part of the history of Chichester, would not have been achieved without the commitment and support of John McKerchar, the Chairman and the Governors of the Oliver Whitby Education Foundation, who agreed to fund the book's publication. Additionally a special word of thanks is due to John McKerchar for Chapter Seven.

I am especially grateful to Dr Geoffrey Barnard, for permission to share his patient and detailed research, together with his thesis on the history of the school. His guidance in reading the manuscript and his corroboration of much that I have written has helped me to bring this book to fruition. The Introduction was contributed by Dr Barnard.

Particular thanks to Noel Osborne, Managing Director, Phillimore & Co. Ltd, whose support for the project is much appreciated.

I am indebted to all Old Boys who have communicated with me their personal stories and experiences, and for having kindly loaned many of the photographs and items of ephemera. In particular I am grateful to Maurice Page and Alan Carter, whose enthusiasm assured me that the project was worthwhile.

I appreciate the help given by the Curator and Archivist at Christ's Hospital together with the kind permission of the Museum and Governors to reproduce the portrait of Oliver Whitby.

It is also a pleasure to acknowledge the support of Freda, Roy and Hugh Spendlove, the daughter and sons of the last Headmaster of the School from 1931 to its closure in 1949. Their attendance at the tercentenary celebrations was much appreciated by Old Boys.

Many friends and relatives of boys who attended the School, and who have been supportive of the project in various ways, Wilfred J. Heath, Michael Merritt (Leader of the 12th Chichester Scout Troop), Jeannette Knott, for permission to quote from her booklet, *Parklands, Chichester* and Jane Windsor, who was Manageress of the Army & Navy Store at the time that they acquired the school building, deserve my sincere thanks.

I would also like to express my appreciation to the Rev. Canon Peter Atkinson for permission to include the Tribute given by Dr G.L. Barnard on the occasion of the Special Choral Service held in Chichester Cathedral on 19 February 2002, marking the anniversary of the death of Oliver Whitby, and to the Rev. John Fox for permission to reprint the Order of Service for this occasion.

Finally I acknowledge the help received from the staffs of the following public bodies: the libraries of Hadleigh, Ipswich and Chichester, West Sussex Record Office, Chichester District Museum, Weald and Downland Open Air Museum and Pallant House, Chichester.

The Nineteenth of February 2002
A PRELUDE

On this day, 19 Old Boys, with their relatives, the daughter and sons of the last Headmaster (Freda, Hugh and Roy Spendlove), together with many other friends having connections to the Old School, met in Chichester to celebrate the tercentenary of the death of Oliver Whitby. As part of these celebrations a special choral service was held in the Cathedral Church of The Holy Trinity (Order of Service, Appendix ix), where the following Tribute was given by Dr Geoffrey Barnard, Former Communar of Chichester Cathedral.

It is clearly a privilege to speak today on the anniversary of Oliver Whitby's death— and it is a daunting task to do justice to the occasion. So here we are then, a remarkable gathering of people, brought together to commemorate not only a school that first saw the light of day almost three hundred years ago, but, more particularly, to hold in grateful remembrance that young man—Oliver Whitby, the Founder. Of course we are sad that the school—'just across the road'—no longer exists in one sense, but the spirit of the founder survives: and that's what really matters. What, however, is most frustrating is the fact that we know so little about Oliver Whitby himself. We know about his father—that Royalist Archdeacon, kicked out from his London parish. by those wretched 'Parliament Men' and, narrowly missing assassination when, having been put in charge of Petworth parish by his friend Bishop Henry King, a 'terrorist' took a pot-shot at him.

But of our Oliver, the Archdeacon's son and only surviving child, there is so little to tell—that he was born in 1664 and died in 1702—that after Winchester and Oxford he finished up in London—and did what? And what prompted him to found a school and, unusually, a fully residential one at that? And why, prescribed in his will, navigation as part of the curriculum? Founding schools for the poor wasn't so uncommon three hundred years ago and there was increasing national interest in navigation, reflecting as it did the post-Restoration extension of world trade and the growth of the Navy—all much inspired by that great Secretary of the Admiralty and diarist, Samuel Pepys on the one hand and, not merely encouraged, but financially supported by an endowment by Charles II of the 'Mathematical School', grafted on to Christ's Hospital—then in London and now, of course, in Horsham, and, as things have turned out, since the 1950s intimately connected with Oliver Whitby. Perhaps in the future, through the wonder of web-sites, the internet *et al.* we shall discover that our Oliver worked alongside Pepys—or even, when living in London, was 'just around the corner' from that other Blue Coat School—Christ's Hospital. But, to encompass the life of the school, what a span of years we look back over—three centuries— three hundred years. Bach and Handel barely fifteen years old when Whitby died. And looking back over that considerable span of 300 years, so many wars: 1939-45; 1914-18;

South Africa; the Crimea; Waterloo. And kings and queens coming and going—six Georges—one Victoria—America lost—Australia found—the interior of Africa explored by Livingstone and others—Chichester's spire falls in—Crystal Palace is built and later moved. And steam drives ships—and petrol engines replace horses.

But can we now, in this year 2002, begin to imagine how those first 12 boys felt on the day they assembled in 1712 at their new school? We know that of the four boys from Harting, two were but eight years old and the other two, nine and 10 respectively. Three of them were described as 'very poor' whilst the fourth was simply 'poor'. But think. How did they get to the school?—by foot?—by pack-horse?—by farm cart to a City that, I guess, none of them had ever visited before and which, in W.H. Auden's words in his poem 'The Night Mail', seemed 'further than Edinburgh or Rome'. They left their village, Harting, and its great spired church—'the Cathedral of the Downs' as it is often called—exchanging it for Chichester's cathedral and its soaring spire. And they met their four comrades from West Wittering about whom, alas, we know nothing. But they, too, had a fine, towered church of some distinction and, moreover, a manor house—Cakeham with its Tudor brick tower—all once the property of the Bishops of Chichester. And did those West Wittering boys ever climb the rickety worm-eaten stairs of that tower and gaze out to sea and dream dreams? And did they compare what they heard went on in that great house at Cakeham with the stories their new Harting friends told of Uppark and the philanderings of its aristocratic owners? And did their Chichester friends and fellow scholars—those comparatively street-wise city slicker—see them as country bumpkins? Or were they brought together by fear—or excited anticipation as, before going to sleep—two to a feathered bed (with blanket and sheets)—they used 'the two forms to sit by the fire on' that the Trustees had bought for the boys' comfort for the princely sum of eight shillings! But one thing was common to them all: they were poor. Moreover, none was a Dissenter and all, as required by the Trustees, were 'healthy and strong and free from the evil, scaled heads, the itch—and falling sickness!

Today, those little boys' successors here present look back, and, as Tennyson writes, 'revolve many memories'—memories of up-days and down-days, of friendships made and lost—of things learnt and example given—of order and discipline—of joy and sorrow; all that made for a life that Old Boys recall today. Many, too, will mourn the the fact that the building across the road is no longer a place of learning—in a traditional sense.

But now I must enter a note of caution! I had a great aunt who was born in the year of the Great Exhibition of 1851 and who lived to be not much short of a hundred! Remarkably, she had little or no patience with those who, in her words, were 'always harking back'— and here we all are, understandably doing what we shouldn't be doing—harking back! Fine! Great to reminisce! Wonderful to meet old friends—face to face—or if not actually here, via web-sites and e-mails and faxes—and no sin to feel sad that the Old School is no more. But what we should be doing, and perhaps, we are, is having in mind Oliver Whitby's vision of opportunity. His spirit and his vision live on through and in the work of the Educational Foundation and its scholarships to Christ's Hospital. Isn't it great that a few boys and girls can still wear that silver breast badge of Strength and Wisdom. Yes, the front door across the road is bolted and barred and leads to nowhere. The Foundation, through its work, is however, able to provide, again in Tennyson's words, 'an arch where-through gleams that un-travelled world'.

That young Royalist Oliver Whitby had a vision. For 250 years boys from Chichester, West Wittering and Harting lived and learnt in the shadow of this great church. Today, at Christ's Hospital that vision is kept alive. Long may it be so!

If you will allow me one minute longer, I would like to add a postscript. Oliver Whitby, in 1678, saw a new organ go up, there, on the screen. At the top of the present case we can still see those same red and gold pipes that he both saw and heard. Oliver Whitby's scholars heard those pipes sounding for 250 years—just as we have today—324 years on! How is that for continuity—and tradition?

Old Boys, taken outside the School's main entrance on the occasion of the three hundredth anniversary, celebrating the life of Oliver Whitby, 19 February 2002. At the back from left to right: Bob Ide, 1946-9; John Haffenden, 1945-9; Dennis Rogers, 1941-6; Doug Baker, 1937-41. Second Row from the back: Ralph Lawrence, 1942-9; Alan Carter, 1941-6; Doug Dibley, 1933-9. Third row from the back: Peter Hughes, 1945-9; Eric Burnand, 1946-9; Bob Burnand, 1936-41; Jack West, 1932-6; Peter Fletcher, 1938-40; Alf Shippam, 1934-9. First row: Maurice Page, 1943-8; Les Burnand, 1942-6; Bob Jellett, 1931-5; Stewart Trodd, 1929-34; Ted Dearling, 1932-6; Ernest Weller, 1933-7.

List of Subscribers

Roy (Dusty) Ashman
Rosemary Aves
D.C. Baker
Eric Bassett
David Beveridge (Oliver Whitby scholar at CH 1953 to 1962)
Dr John Birch
Laura J. Bristol
The Ven. J. Michael Brotherton, Archdeacon of Chichester
Dr Ronald Brown
C. & R. Bryan
Mrs M.M. Bryder (*née* Page)
Eric W. Burnand
Les Burnand
Robert Burnand
Chichester Cathedral Library
Chichester District Museum
Alan G.B. Carter
The Revd Victor Cassam
Freda Chitty (*née* Spendlove)
Mr C.H. Curtis
Captain A.J. Davies, RN
Rosemary Shires Dawe
S.J. Dearling
Kathleen Devonport (*née* Hawkins)
Doug Dibley
David Evershed-Martin
Susan Evershed
Peter (Swampy) Fletcher
Paul Foster
Mrs A.B. George
Cllr Mrs Valerie Gostling
A.H.J. Green
John Haffenden
Nigel Hanbury
Revd Colin Harding
Wilfrid Heath

W.T.G. Huggins
Robert G. Ide
Robert Jellett
David (Jockles) Johnson
Mrs Barbara Laming
Ralph James Lawrence
Kim Leslie
Garry Long
Audrey Déla Macfarlane
Michael W. Merritt
Trilby Mills
Noel Osborne
C.F. Page
J.B. Page
L.V. Page
M. Page
M.G. Page
Mike (Philly) Philmore
C.H. Randall
Dennis Edwin Rogers
Anne Scicluna
Alf Shippam
James William Shier
N.D.B. Smith
G. Hugh Spendlove
Mr P.R. Spendlove CVO
R.M. Stenning
Miss M. Stephenson
Mrs W.E. Thomas
Dr Duncan R. Farquhar-Thomson, MB, BS, FRCA
Stewart A. Trodd
Arthur L. Turner
Ernest Charles Weller
Aidan Charles Elliott Wickham
Angela Wickham
J.W.P. Yates
Peter Youatt

Introduction

Oliver Whitby, by the terms of his will, founded a boy's school in Chichester in 1702. It opened its doors in 1712 and functioned until 1949 when economic and other pressures compelled it to close. Throughout the school's life of almost 250 years, it remained a completely independent boarding institution. The number of boys in the school never exceeded fifty-two when, in the 19th century, it was at its most flourishing. Impervious to national changes that manifest themselves today in the continued existence of schools of similar foundation such as the distinguished Blue Coat Schools in Liverpool and Coventry, Chichester's school was, at its outset, somewhat unusual and at the time of its closure, possibly unique.

At the turn of every century there seems to be an upsurge of concern for, and interest in 'Education'. The government elected in 1997 proclaimed 'Education, education, education', a priority with an emphasis on early stages of schooling. In the years around 1900 a concern for a wider availability of secondary schooling filled political minds. Not long after 1800, and inspired by Lancaster and Bell, the need to institute elementary education 'for the Masses' was increasingly canvassed. This progress towards more widely available schooling gave Chichester the impetus for the setting up of the Lancastrian and Central schools both of which survive, in one form or an other, to this day. Lancaster and Bell provided both the means and method for the many and were not unsympathetically regarded by the government. These moves in the early part of the century culminated in the Education Act of 1870.

Earlier and in similar vein, the efforts of the Society for Promoting Christian Knowledge in 1699 were welcomed as a means of improving the educational lot of the poor. In these 'Charity Schools' an education would be given that edged the children away from illiteracy whilst taking care that 'ideas above their station' were not inculcated. At the turn of the 17th century Chichester's churchmen figured quite prominently in the setting up of the S.P.C.K. Among the active supporters and subscribers were the Bishop, John Williams; the Dean, William Hayley and the Treasurer, Thomas Manningham. Assuming that Oliver Whitby continued a reasonably close connection with his native city, the likelihood of the S.P.C.K. being of some influence in his decision to found a 'Charity School' cannot be ignored. It should be remembered, too, that the date of the school's foundation is early in the overall history of the growth of the Charity School Movement. By the time, however, that Chichester's Blue Coat School actually opened in 1712, the flood-tide of the creation of such schools had turned.

Of Oliver Whitby's School there is now little trace other than an imposing building in Chichester's West Street and the presence at Christ's Hospital at Horsham of a small number of pupils who wear the Oliver Whitby badge and the cost of whose education is supported by the Oliver Whitby Educational Foundation.

This tercentenary book seeks to tell the story of Oliver Whitby and his remarkable school, its teachers, matrons, and its pupils. The school's involvement with the City and its moments of prejudice, bigotry and personal antagonisms are chronicled as are the memories and experiences of 'Old Boys' who recall their days at the Oliver Whitby School.

One

Oliver Whitby: Life and Times
1600–1702

Oliver Whitby, founder of the school, the son of Archdeacon Oliver Whitby and Ann his wife, was born in 1664, the year before London's Great Plague. A child of his father's comparative old age, he was the only survivor of the archdeacon's four children. Oliver was baptised in Chichester Cathedral on 14 July 1664 and he died on 19 February 1702, being buried in the family vault in the South Cloister of the Cathedral on 22 February, just 38 years of age.

The Long Roll of Winchester College records the attendance at the school of a Whitby for the years 1678-80. A number of factors substantiate the supposition that this is indeed our Oliver Whitby: the geographical proximity of Chichester to Winchester and the fact that Winchester College was the nearest school of merit; the Prebendal School of Chichester Cathedral, re-founded in 1497, was barely existing at this time. Also the dates of attendance fit well the known dates he was at Oxford.

Oliver Whitby attended Trinity College Oxford, as did his father, matriculated at the age of 16 on 1 March 1680, and was admitted to the degree of Bachelor of Arts in 1684 and also Bachelor of Law in 1690. The Register of the Middle Temple records his enrolment (7 July 1690) as 'son and heir of Oliver Whitby of Chichester, Sussex, clerk, deceased'. There is little information available regarding his life after 1690 though passing references tell us that he was in Harting on Easter Tuesday, 1696, when he signed the minutes of the Easter Vestry. He was also there in 1698, signing the nominations of Anthony Bullicke and Peter Godding to be overseers of the poor. After this date, 1698, we have no record of Oliver Whitby's movements or activities until we find him signing his will on 16 February 1702, and dying on 19 February.

In order to obtain some understanding of events, together with political ideals and religious prejudices of the time, it is relevant to look closer at the life of his father. Oliver Whitby senior had a remarkable and eventful life and knowledge of his father's experiences may well have influenced some of the terms that his son included in his own will governing the setting up of the school.

Archdeacon Whitby, a native of Bedfordshire, was born in 1602 when Elizabeth I was on the throne and Shakespeare had still to write *Othello*, *Lear* and *Macbeth*. By the time Oliver Whitby (senior) went up to Oxford and joined Trinity College in 1619 James I (and VI of Scotland) had since 1603 succeeded to the throne of England. Then through the untimely death of his eldest son, Charles, but a couple of years older than Whitby, became heir apparent and, in 1625 King. So began struggles, both religious and political, in which Whitby's life by accident or design was inextricably involved.

Oliver Whitby Senior, now ordained, was charged in 1642 before the House of Commons as a scandalous Minister, suffering the loss of the cure of his London parish of St Nicholas Olave. Moreover, the *House of Lords Journal* records that he was said 'to have deserted his cure in order to serve in the Royal Army' and to have told prisoners taken by the Cavaliers at Brentford that 'they were damned and Parliament were traitors'.

However, in the same year of 1642 his friend, and noted Royalist, Henry King, had become Bishop of Chichester holding at the same time 'the rich living of Petworth' with Oliver Whitby as his curate. Dr John Walker's *Sufferings of the Clergy* tells that Whitby, 'being a loyalist, was often in danger of his life by the fanatics, one of whom shot at him with a pistol while he was preaching in Petworth. Although the shot missed, to avoid further danger he escaped to a poor house near Petworth living there for some six months. But being discovered by the rebels, he was forced to take refuge for several days in a hollow tree his landlady had shown him and who kept him in food on the pretence of her going to gather wood.'

After 11 years of Cromwell's Commonwealth (1649-60) came the Restoration of the Monarchy with the return of Charles II, Henry King returned to Chichester as Bishop, and Oliver Whitby, his former 'curate', became one of the Canons Residentiary. Both were to find the City somewhat scarred by the Civil War, with the churches of St Bartholomew to the west and that of St Pancras at the east gate severely damaged if not totally destroyed, whilst within the Close itself the Deanery was no more. The Cathedral too had witnessed considerable damage to both fabric and fittings, including the destruction of the organ which stood on the screen that separated the choir from the nave.

Thus Whitby, after years of tribulation, enjoyed the comparative peace of the Cathedral and profited from a variety of livings including Ford, Clymping, Selsey and, significantly, Harting. He was, moreover, Custos or Warden of St Mary's Hospital, the unique Almshouse in St Martin's Square, Chichester, founded in the 12th century. The duties of this office, which he held until his death, included conducting a daily morning service, supervising the welfare of the inmates and being responsible for the accounts. (It was Whitby's attention, or lack of attention, to the administrative details of his office that subsequently involved his widow and son in a long legal action brought by Henry Edes, a prominent Cathedral dignitary, who succeeded him as Custos.) Finally in 1669, Oliver Whitby senior was installed as Archdeacon of Chichester, an office he held for some ten years until his death in 1679. Whilst the exact date of his death is not known, he was buried on 8 August 1679 in a vault in the south cloister of the Cathedral.

Oliver Whitby senior's will gives us little information, apart from his remembering the Cathedral choristers (£5), the poor of the subdeanery (St Peter the Great), Ralph Brideoake and Peter Gunning, formerly bishops of Chichester, his friends Thomas Briggs and Thomas Smith, together with his nephew, Dr Daniel Whitby, who was to inherit his property and lands if his son Oliver did not survive to inherit from his father.

Only 15 years old when his father died, it would be unwise to presume that the young mind of Oliver Whitby junior would have been unduly influenced by stories of 'Roundheads and Cavaliers' regaled by his father, together with his own experiences of the English Republic. Affairs of national and local importance may enable us to gauge what influenced his thinking and put these times into an historic perspective.

For himself, Oliver Whitby junior saw a succession of Whig Parliaments between 1679-81, and the dissolution of a third at Oxford, probably whilst he was there. In the summer of 1679, the same year Whitby senior died, King Charles II was taken seriously ill and there was disturbance in the public mind as to the succession. Parliament did not meet from 1681 until after the King's death in 1685. In the summer of that year Oliver Whitby celebrated his 21st birthday, James succeeded to the throne and the peace of the realm was again disturbed by the news of Monmouth's rebellion, In the year that Whitby took his B.C.L. at Oxford (1687), James II pressed his attacks upon the Anglican church, during which Magdalen College, Oxford, was turned into a Roman Catholic Seminary. In the following year immediate problems were resolved and John Lake, Bishop of Chichester had with others been committed to the Tower, tried and finally acquitted, William of Orange landed at Torbay on 5 November 1688 and, in December, James fled to France.

It was not merely national events that would have occupied the mind and attention of young Whitby. With Chichester his home and the Cathedral Close his immediate environment, events of a more dramatic nature filled the years following his father's death. These local incidents undoubtedly influenced the terms for the future government of the school which he would later draw up in his will.

In 1679 Bishop Carleton had been moved to write to Archbishop Sancroft about the visit to Chichester of the Duke of Monmouth. Wearing 'a scarlet suit' Monmouth was received by 'the great men of our Chichester [who] welcomed with belles and bonfires'. That same night, Saturday 7 February, Dr Edes officiated as the Duke's chaplain, whilst on the Sunday morning the Bishop suffered the humiliation of seeing Monmouth 'ushered into the Deane's seat with a voluntarie on the organ'. Moreover, the Bishop had to listen to Edes who preached a sermon 'which wanted both loyalty, religion and piety' and then 'omitted praying for the King and the Royal Family'. Monmouth's visit ended in a quarrel with the Mayor, William Jennings. All this was a matter of 'common discourse of the Town and Country about us' and, concludes the Bishop, 'is like to continue so long as Dr Edes continues'. Small wonder that in a later letter he describes Dr Edes as 'a furious firebrand', 'a biggot for Cromwell and Rebellion' and one who 'since the time he could bear arms, hath been a soldier under Cromwell and against the late King'.

It is not clear as to the precise cause, but during 1680 Chichester became the scene of considerable military activity and troop movements. The quartering of militia, the raising and disbanding of companies and so forth are recorded. Whether the place was regarded as a potential danger spot in the event of the King's death does not directly emerge, but if indeed the temper of the City politically and ecclesiastically as opposed to the cathedral is judged from earlier comment, then such activity could well fall into the category of what today would be called 'preventative measures'.

In the autumn of 1681 it was recorded that Monmouth would go down to Sussex to spend the winter at Uppark with Ford, Lord Grey of Werke. (Uppark is now a National Trust property in the parish of Harting, of which Oliver Whitby senior had been vicar and in which Ann, his wife, had property.) At this time Jenkins, Secretary of State, received an anonymous letter from Chichester which he, promptly showed to the Lord Chancellor and to the King. The unknown writer records that the inhabitants of the City were 'as factious a sort of people as any in England, and, as far as I can find by their disposition are ready at an hour's warning to serve the Duke of Monmouth and Lord Grey'. Another anonymous letter to Jenkins alleges, 'a store of arms in a great house of Richard Farrington in South Street', a Member in the last Parliament. In the light of this worrying correspondence the King saw fit to approve a search for arms in Chichester. The plan failed, however, for the trap to catch Faringdon was revealed to him by the very person entrusted with the search.

Events within Chichester achieved national prominence during the summer of 1682, when on 6 August Richard Habin 'an informer'—possibly writer of the letters referred to above—suffered a serious attack outside the house of Farrington in South Street. Habin had fled for protection to the Bishop's Palace and there he died.

On the morning of 16 November 1682, there began in London before the Lord Chief Justice, 'the trial of Richard Faringdon accused as an accessory to the murder of Habin'. After much conflicting evidence, he was acquitted for lack of sufficient evidence.

In the meantime Oliver Whitby and his mother continued to live in the Residentiary, witnesses to events within the Cathedral and outside the entrance to the close, but now they became more directly involved in a law suit with a member of the 'fanatic party'. This law suit was with the notorious Dr Henry Edes, who, it will be recalled, succeeded Oliver Whitby's father as warden of St Mary's Hospital in 1679. Apart from his political activities, Dr Edes appears to have made quite a hobby of 'going to the law', if the various cases that are listed in the Public Record Office in his name are to be counted. Having been at loggerheads with Whitby senior in matters political and ecclesiastical, Edes lost no time in bringing into disrepute his predecessor's conduct of the affairs of the Charity of which he now found himself Warden. So he demanded dilapidations from the estate of Whitby senior, on the grounds that the buildings had been allowed to fall into ruinous condition. The records of the hospital do not support or refute the allegations, but today the initials H.E. 1680 can be seen on the great chimney flues of the hall, which might suggest that rebuilding was carried out. Edes also required that all fines, rents and profits which had been misappropriated by his predecessor should be returned to the hospital funds. Whitby's executors refused to entertain the charge and so the law-suit was commenced in Chancery.

Judgement was given against them with leave to appeal to the Archbishop of Canterbury. The Bishop of Chichester wrote to the Archbishop in support of 'widow Whitby's claim', he urged her humility, modesty and peace of mind, while recording Edes's 'envyous behaviour' towards Whitby whilst he was alive. However, the Archbishop found for Edes and on Monday 2 April 1683 Mrs Whitby paid over the sum of £171 14s. 8d. to Dr Edes in the chapel of St Mary's Hospital. Interestingly, among the documents it shows that Edes, for his part, chose to debit the hospital accounts for £277 12s. 5d. This was costs of the case and, to the Dean and Chapter's objecting, he merely observed that the matter was 'hospital business'. These matters and the general behaviour of Dr Edes could not have endeared him to young Oliver Whitby.

Whilst in 1683 the Whitby's private peace was disturbed by the litigation, public peace was again disturbed by yet another and final visit by Monmouth, with more acrimony between the Mayor and some thousand people who gathered at the Market Cross to cheer the Duke. He was conducted to 'Mr Holme's house in South Street, followed by the crowd who 'behaved very tumultuously, wishing the Duke welcome with loud acclamation of joy'. Once more the Duke cocked a snook at the Cathedral and its Bishop. Although attending morning service on the two Sundays whilst in Chichester, he did not stay for the full service when the Bishop's Chaplain preached 'so full a parallel of rebellion and witchcraft' and using

Samuel 15, verse xxiii for his text: 'Rebellion is as the sign of witchcraft and stubborness as iniquity and idolotry. Because thou hast rejected the word of the Lord, he hath also rejected thee from being King.' This caused uproar with some of Monmouth's party who stayed on to curse the preacher.

After the cloak-and-dagger affair concerning the escape of Monmouth in 1683 to Holland through Chichester harbour, Thomas Carr, later to be one of the first Trustees of Oliver Whitby School, wrote to his brother-in-law in London telling him of the searches for arms and indeed for Monmouth himself, in the houses of Dr Edes and John Peachey. The master of the boat *Hare*, which in all probability took Monmouth and Lord Grey to Holland, was said to be 'a very noted man, ... with a wooden leg, a conventicle preacher'.

Charles II died on 6 February 1685 and James, Duke of York, was crowned. Monmouth, after one last feeble attempt, in the West Country, to usurp the throne, was led to the scaffold and his death on 15 July of that same year.

It can, therefore, be appreciated that the latter years of Oliver Whitby's youth were filled with events both in the national and local arena that must have exercised his mind considerably, especially if he was driven to make contrasts and comparisons with the sufferings of his father some forty years earlier.

1 Facsimile of the first page of Oliver Whitby's will.

Two

The Will and Foundation of the School
1702-1712

The Will of Oliver Whitby, by standards of the time, was quite a sophisticated document, hand written on three large pages of vellum in an 18th-century classical hand. Duly signed and sealed by Whitby on 16 February 1702 in the presence of Robert Smith, George Rutterley, Katherine Chappell and Elizabeth Clayton. He appointed as executors of his will his brother-in-law Thomas Holt of Streatham, Surrey and Francis Goater of Chichester, citizen and alderman. They were required by the will to see that his body was buried in the family vault within the great cloister of Chichester Cathedral and that 'a decent monument' be erected to the memory of his father, his mother and himself. For this an expenditure of £50 was authorised. This monument still exists today within the south cloister.

The minor bequests of Oliver Whitby's will are interesting in that they demonstrate his comparative prosperity. He left £40 each to his cousin Daniel and sister Anne, £20 each to two other cousins, £10 to yet another cousin and to a Margaret Hall. His friend Francis Goater and executor received £10, his servant James Terry, £5 per annum, £8 to the poor of Harting and £5 to the poor of both West Wittering and Chichester. These bequests were to be distributed within one week of his death.

As was customary for the times, the will included instructions for the distribution of linen and also two pleasant bequests, one 'my little purse of old gold and Edward shillings and suit of monye' to his niece, Anne Holt. The remainder of his books to Francis Salisbury, whose father had succeeded Oliver Whitby senior as Vicar of Harting in 1680.

Our main concern, however, is with that part of the will which determined the founding and nature of the school. In summary, Oliver Whitby endowed or founded a school 'for the maintenance of a master and 12 poor boys, to be carefully educated in the principles of religion as established in the Church of England; and also to be diligently instructed in reading, writing and arithmetic, and as far in mathematical learning as may fit them for honest and useful employment with regard to navigation'.

There are more detailed instructions for his executors, perhaps the best interpretation of which is contained in The Report of the Commissioners on the Education of the Poor of 1819. Whitby

gave to his Trustees his messuage lands and tenements in the parish of West Wittering in the County of Sussex, and also the rectory and parsonage of West Wittering, and all his estate term and interest therein, upon special trust that the said Trustees should out of the estate so devised to them (as soon as conveniently might be) purchase a convenient messuage or dwelling house in some convenient place within the city of Chichester, to be settled for ever for the school-house and place of habitation for the master and 12 poor boys or scholars; which should from time to time be chosen out of the poor boys whose parents were not dissenters, and were exempt from the poor tax, to be chosen within the city of Chichester and the parishes of Harting and West Wittering, four from each place, if boys fitting should be offered. And the testator willed that the said master and scholars should all have their diet in the said school-house, and also a convenient servant for them; and that the master should have for his teaching and instructing the said 12 boys, over and besides his lodging and diet in the school-house, the clear yearly sum of £20 per annum, paid him quarterly without any deduction, for which he should teach the 12 boys writing, arithmetic and the mathematics; and that all the said boys should be allowed blue gowns, with the crest of his coat of arms in some sort of metal affixed thereto for a badge, and quilt caps, which they should constantly wear; and that there should be yearly allowed 20 shillings for every boy to buy the gowns and caps, and other such apparel as shoes and stockings as the 20 shillings per annum for each boy would extend to. And he gave power to his Trustees to make rules and orders for the government of the master and boys, and to displace the master and choose a new one who should always be one of the communion of the Church of England, and also to displace any of the boys.

An important clause of the will was with regard to the Trustees of the school. Whitby nominated as his first Trustees his two executors, Thomas Holt and Francis Goater with Thomas Carr 'of the Pallant', a noted 'Tory' and George Gounter of Racton (a small village near Harting). They were empowered to elect to their board, in order to maintain their number at five, but Whitby stipulated in his will that they shall not choose any 'parliament man or dissenter', so ensuring that only supporters of the monarch and followers in the faith of the Church of England would oversee his wishes. (Gounter's father George had helped in the escape of Charles II and the *Royal Oak* at Racton is still regarded as one of the places where the King stayed.)

(An interesting subsidiary provision was that the Trustees should from time to time pay for the teaching of six poor children of the parish of West Wittering to read, and to buy them necessary books.)

Oliver Whitby's school has generally been called a Charity School. If the time of its foundation is considered then within the terms of the endowment, it may loosely be called such. Whilst it is true to say that the school had many features in common with the Charity School proper, it is equally true that it had qualities that made it markedly different.

At the turn of the 18th century there was little provision for 'elementary' education throughout Britain, but it would be wrong to assume there was no 'primary' education. In the reign of Queen Anne 1702-14, charity schools were founded all over England to educate the children of the poor in reading, writing, moral discipline and the principles of the Church of England. Such schools were much needed, as the State did nothing at this time for the education of the poor, although in many villages 'dames' and other unofficial persons taught rustics their letters in return for small fees. In some places there were endowed Grammar Schools which gave secondary education to a limited number. It is possible that the early development of the Charity Schools did influence Whitby in his thinking and planning. It could be said his school anticipated the main movement and his plans may have been intended as a prototype of some sort of 'higher' Charity School. His trustees, however, based their rules and articles of government for the school on standard charity school practice. The date of Whitby's will is early in the history of the Charity School movement and arguably the specific terms may suggest that he had in his mind some sort of 'higher' education.

The setting up of charity schools will always be synonymous with the S.P.C.K. (Society for Promoting Christian Knowledge). Lowther Clarke's *History of the S.P.C.K.* makes it clear that the idea of a charity school was not entirely new and cites the Red Maids, Bristol 1634 and Grey Coat School, Westminster 1698 as examples. However, the Society's minutes of 8 March 1699 are significant, for on that day it was resolved 'to further and promote the good Design of erecting Catechiticall Schools in each parish in and about London'. Interestingly the first school established outside London was at Chester in 1701.

Although it would perhaps be gratifying to record that Whitby was immediately involved in those early days of the S.P.C.K. and the setting up of charity schools, alas no record of formal connection exists. What is interesting to note, however, is that in the short list of first members enrolled, four are prominent members of the Chichester Chapter, namely John Williams, the Lord Bishop, William Hayley, the Dean, Thomas Manningham, the Treasurer and William Barcroft. It must be within the bounds of possibility, even probability, that an influence from the cathedral circle, so well known to him, would have been a deciding factor in his decision making. Whitby may have even had some unofficial or indirect involvement through these clerics, with the Society, but this is pure supposition. Nevertheless, whatever else his school was, it was an early example of a charity school, judged by any standard.

Whitby's foundation, apart from its being a comparatively early endowment, was also a school with a difference. That difference is in the expressed desire or intention that mathematics should be taught. Although in itself not original, the combination at such an early date of 'charity school' plus 'mathematical school' is certainly rare. The interest in the teaching of mathematics, with particular regard to navigation, reflects not only the importance of the navy which had built up over the past century, but also of the great development of sea-borne trade with the consequent demand for officers trained in navigation. As early as 1679 Dartmouth Grammar School provided a master to teach the art of navigation and other mathematics. Other examples include: Sir John Williamson's Mathematical School at Rochester, 1701 and Neale's Mathematical School in Fetter Lane London, opened in 1715. The most notable example is the Mathematical School at Christ's Hospital, which dates from 1673.

The importance of instruction in navigation was a constant theme in letters to Samuel Pepys who had been elected to parliament in 1679 and appointed Secretary to the Admiralty. Pepys-Halley correspondence in 1695-6 repeatedly stresses 'imperfect attainments in the art of navigation'. Hamstead, a correspondent of Pepys, writing in 1697, declares, 'Tis vain to expect that so long as our Navys are supply'd with unthrifts or ungovernable spirits the Science of navigation should improve; it will decay and impair if you bring not youth better educated than our common saylors usually are, into your Fleets. If we had many such seminarys of young seamen as that at Christ's Hospital is and those such masters as well able and careful to teach them the true grounds of Geography and Navigation,' all would be well. Later, reference is made to Christ's Hospital as a seminary 'for Able Seamen' [sic] and the hope is expressed that some from that and other such schools 'might rise to command'. (Samuel Pepys, became a governor of Christ's Hospital in 1676.)

Whitby's will undoubtedly reflects the religious and political implications of the charity school movement and, although there were feelings voiced that these schools had been founded and were run by the church and largely Tory sympathisers, in the main the schools were accepted. *The Spectator* 6 February 1711 declared them as 'laudable institutions' and the movement as such as 'primarily a middle class and Puritan movement, consecrating wealth to God, accepting social inequalities in his will and with no idea of altering the social fabric.'

One thing was clear, Whitby was going to have no truck with Dissenters either as masters or pupils in his school, or as his Trustees. Neither was he going to have a 'Parliament Man' as a Trustee. It is likely that 'Parliament Man' for Whitby evoked and enshrined all the memories of the forces of anti-king and establishment that he knew second-hand from his father, together with the intrigue and bloodshed he had been witness to in his youth and early manhood. If indeed Whitby was so strictly limiting in his will then his Trustees soon elected to the board Sir John Miller, who was a Member of Parliament for Chichester. Similarly, his attitude to 'Dissenters' is understandable in the light of his own background and experience.

With regard to other aspects of the foundation and endowment, Oliver Whitby's school has some features outside the normal pattern. In the first place it was an endowed school in the sense that it had a permanent income derived from a bequest, in this case the estate of the founder. Although not unique—for example, there were Kilmersdown in Somerset; Luton, which by the will of John Pierrepoint, had an estate. worth £306 per annum; Shinfield, with an endowment of £42 per annum; and also Dunchurch in Warwickshire, an estate to build a school house for the master and family and endowed with £36 per annum—but these schools were in the minority. The essential features of the financing of the charity schools proper were the subscription list and the collection taken at charity sermons. Maintenance by these annual subscriptions rather than by large individual bequests was common. This 'begging for alms' as it were, was to become an object of criticism. However, those responsible for the charity school movement added to the principle of endowment, the new idea of co-operation. No longer was patronage and support to rest with a few wealthy and generous people, but the principle of small subscriptions and donations was to be exploited to the full. The parish was the focal point and the shopkeeper or humble artisan were persuaded to take more than a passing interest in something that they themselves had provided.

In the archives of the S.P.C.K., the almost endless publications of Charity Sermons helped to edify the prospering middle class, as did the grand parades of the charity children attending weekly and annual services at city churches. The present-day annual parade through London by the scholars of Christ's Hospital continues the tradition. Specially composed hymns, one of which Oliver Whitby's school proudly possesses, were sung. Likewise the wearing of uniforms not only identified but made these children from very poor homes respectable. This would please the benefactors by a visible token of their generosity and would help in preserving discipline out of school. If the subscribers were eager to do their part, the poor were not always as eager to partake of the benefits as a letter from Whitby's cousin, Gilbert White of Selborne, written to the S.P.C.K. in 1710 tells that many of his subscribers had withdrawn 'by reason of the inconstancy of the poor in sending their children to school'.

A factor perhaps unique to the Chichester school was a specific instruction of Whitby's with regard to dress. A gown and cap were standard dress for Charity Schools, but Whitby made the stipulation that the boys were to wear a badge or crest of his arms 'in some sort of metal'. Although in 1713 in the S.P.C.K.'s orders for masters and scholars of Charity Schools mention is made of 'other marks of distinction' additional to the conventional caps, bands and gowns, no specific reference is made to badges in lists of clothing and costs as printed and published. (It has been said, but without authority, that the wearing of badges at Charity Schools was a survival of the earlier custom in connection with workhouse schools.)

With regard to the Arms of Oliver Whitby there is a note taken from Chichester Papers No 4 by L.B. Ellis MA which describes the Arms: 'Argent a chevron sable between in chief two crosses formy fitchy gules, and in a base a coiled serpent vert'. This device is carved with his crest, a tree entwined with serpent above the entrance to the former school building.

Oliver Whitby's school was also unusual in that, by the founder's direction, his scholars were to be 'wholly maintained'. It is clear from his will that the school was to be entirely residential with a place of habitation for the Master and pupils, who are to have all their diet and a servant to look after them. We can only conjecture as to precise implications with regard to the servant. The school could not have been anything but residential since the pupils were to come from Harting, 13 miles to the north, and Wittering, seven miles to the south, as well as from Chichester itself. (The term 'wholly maintained' only appears in one other entry in the Account of Charity Schools for 1713, that is at Kingston-upon-Hull, Yorkshire, where there was a 'School or Workhouse' where the children were 'wholly maintained and taught to write, read and spin wool'.)

Although Oliver Whitby's School cannot be called unique, it certainly had features that were less common for the time. Above all its early conception, advanced curriculum and the complete residential nature are of importance. Each in its way plays a part in the subsequent history of the school.

2 The original School building, 52 West Street, Chichester, which the Trustees first rented in 1712 and subsequently purchased in 1721. The roof tablet reads: 'Charity-school founded by Oliver Whitby, Esq., A.D. 1702'. This picture was probably taken in 1904 prior to the demolition and rebuilding of the School on the same site.

Three

The Eighteenth and Nineteenth Centuries
1712-1870

Although founded in 1702 the school did not in fact open until June 1712. Presumably the trustees resolved to build up some capital before attempting the opening of the school. The elected treasurer, Francis Goater, having spent six shillings on an account book, recorded all money received by him from the several lands and tenements in West Wittering. Each year the trustees met and passed Goater's accounts until at the beginning of 1712 when, according to the *The Account of Charity Schools*, it is noted that 'for want of a Stock to begin work, [the opening of the school] has been delayed till 1712 when there was about 1000L. [approximately £94,600 at current value] in Bank.' With this capital the trustees felt able to embark upon the serious business of opening their school.

By this time the tide of the Charity School movement was in full flood and educational provision in Chichester had improved. In 1710, following the national example, Charity Schools were set up in Chichester, the first being a Grey Coat School for boys, the Master of which was a Robert Clarke. From the Grey Coat School Accounts and the Whitby Account Book we learn that Francis Goater appears as a trustee of both schools and that the same Robert Clarke was appointed the first Master of Oliver Whitby's school in 1712. He held both these appointments simultaneously receiving £20 per annum for each office.

In 1713 the 'Account of Charity Schools' records for Chichester: '3 Schools lately erected, one for 30 Boys which are clothed, taught to read, write cost Accompts, and to repeat the Catechism. The Subscription is about 60L. per Annum. Another for 20 Girls clothed, taught to read, write and work with the needle, the subscription about 40L. per Annum. Another school for 12 Boys taught Writing, Arithmetic and the Mathematicks, clothed and wholly maintained by an Estate of 150L. Per Annum.' The latter is clearly Oliver Whitby's school. However, in the following year (1714), mention is made of only two schools, one for girls and the other 'for 42 Boys'. The 'Account' which records this does note that 12 of the boys are on the Whitby Foundation and that their education has a 'difference'. Having a common master suggests that the schools functioned as a single unit, but we do not know where the Grey Coat School met and it is possible that the house eventually used for the Whitby scholars was in fact simply their place of habitation, and they joined forces with the Grey Coat boys for teaching purposes.

The Oliver Whitby trustees were enjoined to purchase a house, but in fact they did not do so initially, but were content to rent one for £15 per annum (at current value £1,420). This house belonged to the late Randolph Tutte and was on the north side of West Street, opposite the Cathedral. Having acquired a house, their next concern, after carrying out some minor repairs, was to furnish it and an inventory was made as follows:

	£	s.	d.
One Copper Furnace to play a Hogshead	[		]
One [-] to Mash 12 Bushells with good Oakern hoops	2		
[-] Hogsheads Iron Bound	1		
One powdering Tub to Salt a quarter of Beefe	0	10	0
Seaven Bedsteads Matts and Cords	4	11	0
Seaven Ffeather Beds and Bolsters	12	5	0
One and Twenty Blanketts	5	5	0
Seavan Coverletts	4	4	0
Table Clothes and Towells	1	10	0
One good strong long Oaken Table (*Now at Christ's Hospital*)		14	0
Two good Oakern fforms		12	0
Two fforms and a Desk for ye School (*For use in Grey Coat School?*)	1	10	0
Two Picture fframes		5	0
Two Dozen of Pewter Plates	1	0	0
Six Pewter Chamber poets		15	0
Six Pewter Dishes	1	4	0
One dozen of Ockemy Spoons		3	0
Twelve Knives and a box		7	0
One Large Copper Boyler	1	5	0
One Lesser Boyler		10	0
One Large Range to Bum Coals in	1	15	0
Two small Oaken Tables for ye Chambers		12	0
Twelve Oaken Boxes with Locks and Keys	2	8	0
One pottle [½ gallon] Copper drinking pott and two ½ pints.		10	0
Two fforms to Sitt by the fire on		8	0

Two interesting points arise from this list: firstly, the provision of boxes for the boys to lock up their personal goods, primarily, we must presume, clothes, as it is unlikely that, as poor boys, they would have anything of value. Secondly, it is clear that the number of boys to be admitted was 12, although, in the matter of bedding, only seven and multiples thereof are detailed. We can only speculate and presume they had double beds with the odd one being for the servant. As may well have been the practice at this time, two boys slept in the same bed with a head at each end, which would also have provided a modicum of warmth.

In May the electing of scholars, which was in the hands of the parishes concerned, took place. The Harting Vestry meeting, on 2 May 1712 'for nominating and electing four poor boys to be sent to ye Charity School at Chichester' chose as the first to benefit from their locally connected benefactor:

Wm Bennet	a Poor Orphan	aged abt. 10 years
Tho Wood	a very poor boy	aged abt. 10 years
Tho Pearcey	a very poor boy	aged abt. 9 years
John Hill	a very poor boy	aged abt. 8 years

It is not known who was elected from West Wittering as no records exist but there is a clue as to two of the four Chichester boys which may well indicate the nature and esteem that Oliver Whitby's School was held under at this early time. Robert Clarke, in his role as

Master of the Grey Coat School, made notes in the summer of 1712 on some of his pupils. He expelled three, 'discarded' one, George Purchas (maybe because he had reached the age of 12), and transferred 'Tho. Gruggen aged 11 and John Boots into ye other school'. The higher education of the Whitby foundation may have been attractive or the domestic circumstances of the boys may have warranted their being wholly maintained.

Thus, with a house acquired and equipped, a Master appointed and pupils selected, the first Oliver Whitby scholars assembled in June 1712 in clothing (supplied by a Mr Parker of London) all as their founder had directed. They were also provided with 'Bibles bound with the Common Prayer' and 'Catechisms' for which the sum of £3 1s. 6d. was paid.

Another responsibility of the Trustees was to draw up rules for the government of their school. This they did, calling upon Robert Clarke, the Master, to make a fair copy for them. The 'Articles', as the Trustees chose to call their rules, are as follows:

1) That ye Boys be Twelve in Number betwixt ye Age of 7 and 12. That they be chosen out of ye Poore from time to time whose parent are not Dissenters, and are by reason of their poverty, exempt from ye Poor Tax.

2) That they be chosen out of ye City of Chichester, ye Parishes of Harting and West Wittering, from either place 4 if Boys fitting be offered, otherwise to be supplyed out of either of ye places aforesaid.

3) That ye boys be allowed all their Dyet, together with a Convenient servant to mend their Cloths and keep clean and neat.

4) The ye Boys shall be taught and Instructed in writing Arithmetic and ye Mathematicks.

5) That ye Boys be allowed Blew Gowns with ye Crest of the Ffounders Coat of Arms Cast in some sort [of] mettle affixed thereunto for a Badge, Quilt Caps which [they] shall constantly wear.

6) That there be allow'd Twenty Shillings for every Boy yearly to buy ye sd. Gownes and Caps and such apparrell as stockings Shoes and c as ye said Twenty Shillings p Annum for each Boy shall extend to.

Order'd always to keep up the Number of Five Trustees. [*This line is added in a hand other than Clarke's, and makes immediate record of the founder's precise intention as expressed in his will.*]

7) That no Boys be Admitted, but such as are Healthy and Strong ffree from distempers as ye Evill, Scalld heads, Itch, Falling Sickness and ye like to which end ye Trustees shall carefully view and examin them before their admission.

8) That in ye Election of Boys regard be First principally had to Orphans, and in ye next place to such as have most Children and least to Maintain them with, and are in all respects qualified according to Article ye first.

9) The ye Boys chosen in ye City have leave to visit their Friends once a Week or oftener but not suffre'd to stay one night with them.

10) That every Morning before Breakfast and in ye Evening before Supper, a Chapter be read and a prayer which is compos'd for them be said in ye Publick School, by one of ye Boys (each to take his day in turn) with the Grace said before and after Breakfast, Dinner and Supper. And after Supper ye Boys to sing a Psalm. And on Sunday nights, their Supper and Exercise to be publick, that any of ye Town or Strangers may be present and to conclude with one of the Boys makeing a publick Thanksgiveing to God for the Benefaction bestowed upon them.

11) Every Tuesday and Fryday in ye Evening ye Boys to be Catechised.

12) The Boys to go to ye Morning Prayers at the Subdeanery and in ye Evening to ye Choir. Order'd also, that a Box is set up in ye Hall, with a Blew Coat Boy painted over it to receive the Benevolence of Strangers and Visitors.

Examination of typical and suggested orders for the general run of schools and printed in the 1713 Accounts of Charity Schools makes interesting comparison. In the first place the Master of the Charity School must be 'a member of the Church of England, of sober life and conversation and not under the age of 25 years'. As far as the Whitby Foundation was concerned this rule went without saying.

At the time the school opened the age for Whitby's scholars parallels the national pattern. Charity children were to be fully seven years old and not above twelve years and the school records show no change in this school leaving age before the 19th century. Most orders stipulated teaching hours, but no mention is made of this for Whitby's school, presumably because of its residential nature.

The S.P.C.K. in their orders remind the Master of the 'chief design of the school', as 'the Education of Poor Children in the Knowledge and Practice of the Christian Religion as Profess'd and Taught in the Church of England'. This clearly inspired the Whitby trustees' title page to their 'Articles'. The boys are 'to be Instructed in the Christian Religion as professed in ye Church of England', and two quotations from the scriptures to remind the Master, on the one hand, that he should 'Train up a Child in ye way he should goe; and when he is old he will not depart from it' (*Proverbs, 22 v.6*), and enable the trustees, on the other hand, to be pleased in the assurance that 'Blessed is he that considereth ye por and needy: the Lord shall deliver him in the time of trouble.' (*Psalm 41 v.1*) The title page of the Whitby 'Articles' also states that the purpose of education is to fit the boys 'for Imployment for the benefit of themselves and the Kingdom'.

The saying of prayers morning and evening, reciting of grace at meals and the regular attendance at church are common in the S.P.C.K. orders and the Whitby 'Articles'. The trustees stipulate morning service at the 'Subdeanery' and evening prayer in the 'Choir'. (Chichester Cathedral at this time had within it a 'parish church' in its own right consisting of what is now the Treasury and extending westwards into the North Transept.) This practice ceased in the middle of the 19th century when the Church of St Peter the Great was built almost opposite the Cathedral and adjacent to the Oliver Whitby school. Whitby boys, in fact, went every Sunday morning to the Cathedral up to the closing of the school in 1949, although it is not known when they ceased attending evening prayer.

Because of the entirely residential nature of the school a number of the Whitby 'Articles' are unique or uncommon for charity schools in general. One such Article was the provision of the 'convenient servant'. The trustees, for their part, imply that the servant's main duties were to care for the clothes and appearance of the boys rather than of a more domestic nature. Research confirms this supposition from the fact that an early 'servant' of the school, Mary Hollingsworth, appears in the register of Sussex Apprentices and Masters as a 'seamstress' and some six years later as 'housewife'.

'Article 10' requires 'Supper and Exercise to be publick that any of ye Town or Strangers may be present'. Many motives were probably behind this article. The idea of throwing the doors open to the public for examination was not uncommon. Perhaps the boys were required to display their new-found knowledge in Arithmetic and Mathematics. Moreover, this not uncommon practice would also serve to demonstrate the efficiency of the master and his charges; gave opportunity to the Trustees to show forth their zeal and competence and nullified any attempts at a campaign, which might suggest that the children were taught to babble 'High Church' or support the Jacobite cause. Quite simply it would be good for trade, what today we would call marketing, in that the good people of Chichester might be prevailed upon to support this charity school and place handsome gifts in the box provided. It is interesting, however, to note that at no point do the accounts of the school record any miscellaneous income which might be assumed to have come from any such collection box.

Reconstructing the daily life and routine of Oliver Whitby's School at this time is dependant almost entirely upon the Minutes of the Trustees and their Account Book. There is additional information derived from correspondence of local residents at the time, but this is allusive and not of prime importance. Nevertheless some small impression of this residential charity school emerges.

As could be expected, many entries in the Account Book are routine. For example, the regular payment to the Master of his £5 per quarter (at current value £473) for teaching and the cost of board of the 12 boys, which at the outset was £20 (at current value £1,893) per quarter, remain constant for the first decade or so. Likewise, Edward Barnard, the Dean's verger, collects a pew-rent of one shilling a head per annum for a seat in the Cathedral. The boys were bought gloves every Christmas. New 'pudding pans' and a kettle were purchased, work was done 'about the oven and ffurnace', the cesspits were emptied and an ironing cloth was bought. The window-tax was paid annually and incredibly large recurrent sums of money were paid to John Hammond, glazier, for repairing the windows in the school rooms (e.g. 19 shillings in 1714; £1 5s. in 1715; £1 14s. in 1716). It is not clear whether the windows were broken from within or without, probably both. But a local historian, William Spershott, born in 1710, and writing his memoirs in the late 18th century, casts some light on the scene at the early part of the century. He lists 'among the diversions of the commonality'—'Bullbaiting, wrestling, cudgeling, footballing in the streets, day after day in frosty weather, to the advantage of the Glazier.' Added to this was the fact that within the City wall at the time Chichester had 49 public houses and that it was not uncommon for farmers when they came to the markets, one of which which was held in West Street outside the front door of Oliver Whitby's, to get drunk and stay two or three days until their wives came to fetch them home. So it is easy to see the windows of the school being an attractive target for the 'commonality'. Bearing this in mind, it seems odd that it took almost 150 years before the Trustees saw fit to protect their windows rather than repair them. In 1860, Alfred Rasell, wire worker, was paid £1 16s. for wire work to protect the school windows.

As far as educational equipment is concerned there is limited information available. Joseph Lee, bookseller, provided an endless supply of catechisms and also paper two or three times a year, which is described in the accounts variously as 'fine paper' or 'fooles cap thick paper'. Robert Clarke, the Master, is reimbursed 18s. 4d. for mathematical instruments for use in the school and similarly a payment to a Simon Scatliff for £1 7s. No mention is made of the nature of the instruments nor does the Sussex list of Masters and Apprentices indicate Scatliff's trade. In 1715 Francis Mitten, clock maker of St Pancras, was paid 4s. 'for mending two Globes'.

Despite the attempts by the Trustees to ensure the fitness of the boys upon their entering the school, nothing could prevent their falling victims to the common diseases of the time. In the year 1714-15 the Master received reimbursement of £6 6s. 11½d. when eight charity boys had the smallpox. Likewise an expenditure of £1 10s. is recorded 'for a charldron of Sea cole as an allowance for the ffiar [fire] kept extraordinary'. In the following year the boys had the measles, which proved less expensive, for Robert Clarke's extraordinary expenditures were only £1 2s. 6d. and medicines £1 3s. 0d.

The Trustees, for their part, made efforts to improve the financial position of the Foundation's funds. Money was lent usually at an interest of five per cent and minor sums were derived from the sale of timber cut on the 'Charity Farm', at West Wittering; for example, £36 being received for '345 ffoot of Elm Timber cut by Henry Steel'. The task of selecting timber appears to have been quite a pleasure for the Trustees as it is recorded that they went to Wittering by coach, twice in six months, to view and mark the timber to be cut and spending 3s. 0¾d. on each occasion 'for Brandy, Lemons and Sugar for Punch'. However, these 'modest' expenses made no significant inroads upon the capital of the trust and Whitby's desire for a house to be bought for his school was fulfilled. The house in West Street, which had been rented since the school's opening, was bought for a sum of £300 0s. 0d. paid in two instalments with John Wakeford, the Chapter Clerk, acting for and on behalf of the Trustees. So, on 9 February 1721 the Oliver Whitby school was properly housed on its own site and remained there for 228 years.

Over the next few years life at the school appears to have settled into a steady routine. The accounts show us that the windows continued to be repaired and ink, pens and paper were bought. The charge for the use of seats in the Cathedral was reduced firstly to 10s. and subsequently to 8s. The boys were again struck down with smallpox, which in Chichester peaked in 1722 with 168 recorded deaths from the disease, a distressing year for the city the population of which at this time was only just above three thousand. An entry showing Mr Clarke being paid £5 6s. 0d. 'for teaching the Boys when they had the Small Pox for Wine and other necessaries' may support the view that in normal circumstances the Grey Coat boys and the Blue Coat boys were taught together, except at times of forced isolation. Unfortunately, the accounts record the first fatality among the boys with the death, from smallpox, of Samuel Lucas. Mary Hollingsworth, the 'servant' or perhaps more appropriately, housekeeper, was reimbursed for her trouble and the boy's funeral expenses: 'a shroud 5s. 6d.: coffin 12s. 0d.: Parson, Clarke Grave and Bell 3s. 6d.: Certificate burying in Woolen 1d.'

At about this time, 1725-6, Goater, the treasurer, saw fit to lend himself £50 from the school accounts, possibly upon his election as an alderman. At the annual meeting of 8 December 1727, those Trustees present noted that no interest is recorded in connection with 'Alderman Goater's loan' to himself. However, lest his fellow Trustees should doubt his integrity, Goater records in the following years accounts, 'Mr Alderman Goater's bill for Physik for the poor children, one of whom, vizt Richard Owton lying Sick some Months, for all which the good Alderman will take only £0 15s. 0d.' There is no record of interest ever being paid and nowhere do the accounts record a repayment of the capital sum!

In 1725 the Trustees decided to follow what was becoming a tradition of Charity Schools—they provided a wooden statue of a Blue Coat Boy for which they paid a Mr Watts £1 4s. 0d. This three-foot statue, subsequently known affectionately as the 'Blew Boy' or 'Carv'd Boy', survived the school and now stands in Christ's Hospital. In its early days it would have spent much of the time outside the front door of the school 'begging' for alms and donations from the kind people of the city. The accounts show an annual expenditure of 5s. for the painting of the statue, which could have been done before being taken into the Cathedral for a Charity Sermon given on behalf of the school. Every boy who attended

Oliver Whitby's will remember the 'Blew Coat' boy; to early scholars 'he' may have given some sense of security, knowing that 'he' was 'working' on their behalf. In later years, after the practice of begging in this way was discontinued and there were no more Charity Sermons, the statue spent many years standing on a magnificent oak staircase in the main school building and many boys will have spent time polishing 'him'. There was the belief that on certain occasions the ghost of an 'old boy' could be heard walking up and down the oak staircase and that this was the statue coming to life. Nobody knows how or when this idea originated, but it was a favourite ruse of older boys to try to frighten new boys and was, as I bear witness, practised until the school closed.

In the spring of 1731 Mary Hollingsworth died and was replaced as 'servant' by Jane Forebench. Whereas Mrs Hollingsworth served the Trustees and the boys faithfully for almost twenty years, her successor survived for little more than twenty months. At an extraordinary meeting of the Trustees on 19 December 1734, she was dismissed since 'it does appear to us that Thomas Forebench and Jane his wife hath not behaved themselves well to us and the Boys'. In their place was appointed Mary Stint to be 'housekeeper and

3   The wooden Blue Coat Boy, almost a metre tall and carved in 1725, when it would have stood outside the front door of the school 'begging' for alms and donations. The oak base was added in 1904, being made from wood recovered from the old school building which was demolished for rebuilding.

Looker over of the said twelve Blue Coate Boys and carefully provide for them as usually and heretofore hath been done'. Interestingly she is no longer referred to as a 'convenient servant'.

This same year 1734, the last of the original Trustees, John Wakeford, had died and Chichester suffered two earthquakes. Whether these events were related or not, the Trustees resolved for the first time to insure the school with the Royal Exchange Fire Office in London against loss and damage. There was a severe storm, a result of which the Trustees visited Wittering to view for sale the timber which had been blown down. Moreover, it is noted that the boys were miserable throughout this summer when 'Oyntment' costing the large sum of £3 failed to cure the boys of 'the Itch'.

One of the hallmarks of the Charity School movement was the system of apprenticing. The S.P.C.K. stressed that one of the aims of education was to fit boys and girls for 'Service and Apprenticeship'. However, there is no evidence of the Trustees of Oliver Whitby's, in the early days of the school, apprenticing the boys at all, let alone to Masters of Ships. This is surprising in view of the proximity of Chichester Harbour with its wharf at Dell Quay, where a flourishing wool and wine trade was carried on. Often a failure to apprentice pupils was the direct result of a lack of finances, but in the case of Oliver Whitby's we assume there was no such problem. There are only two references in the accounts during the first 25 years of the school's existence which could loosely be concerned with apprenticing: in 1731, 'Stephen Linttots indentures to Mr Sherer, £0 8s. 0d.' and in 1737 is recorded 'Paid for Cloths for Anthony Pink and His Carriage and Charges to London £3 3s. 3d.'.

The year 1737 saw the practice of end of term 'treats' starting, whereby the boys were taken to a public performance of music or a play. Old Oliver Whitbyians today recall the practice, still in existence until the final closing of the school, of going to see a film at the end of term, or pantomime at Christmas.

At this time the procedure for entry to the school was changed. In the past, selection had been in the hands of the individual parishes of Harting, West Wittering and Chichester; now we find that nominations were to be given in writing and final selection was to be in the hands of the Trustees and this procedure was followed during the remaining years of the school.

In February 1738 the Trustees implemented another of Oliver Whitby's wishes, that of the boys wearing his badge upon their gowns. They decided that this should be silver for Sunday wearing and white metal for other days.

In the winter of 1740 Chichester was again plagued by another attack of smallpox, with 66 deaths in the City including another Oliver Whitby boy, Thomas Menville. The local apothecary was paid what can only be considered an enormous sum of £12 16s. 9d. for treating the boys. Stepney's fee as doctor in attendance was a mere £2 2s. 0d. There is no direct proof, but the apothecary's high fee may have been due to the boys being inoculated against the smallpox, since it is known that, during this year in Chichester, inoculation was practised.

By the end of the year the 'good alderman Goater', friend of the Founder, keeper of the accounts, minister to the boys in their sickness, had died and by his will the school received £216. Also Henry Peckham was appointed a Trustee; known as 'Mercer' Peckham, he was brother to Henry 'Lisbon' Peckham, the great 18th-century Chichester wine merchant. They both lived in North Pallant but it was 'Lisbon' Peckham who with his wife was responsible for building Pallant House in 1712.

Robert Clarke, who had been Master of the School since its opening, announced his retirement at a meeting of the Trustees in 1749, 'upon Account of his great Age and Infirmities'. It was agreed that an annuity (or pension) of £10 be paid half yearly to Clarke for his services. This set a precedent that was to cause much bitterness later in the 19th century under the rule of less generous Trustees.

The Trustees appointed Israel Killwick, a recommended Chichester schoolmaster, and his wife, to take up the education, care and maintenance of the children. During Clarke's term as Master it is clear that, married or not, a separate servant or housekeeper, in accordance with Whitby's will, had been employed. With the arrival of Killwick the Master's wife was to undertake the domestic management of the school, and subsequently the role of housekeeper became more that of nurse or matron. This pattern prevailed until the closure of the school, when Mrs Spendlove, the headmaster's wife, acted as 'Housekeeper' and latterly as 'Matron'.

With Clarke spanning the first half of the century, the first decades of the history of the school came to an end. The number of boys remained at 12 and, as far as can be determined, the intentions of the Founder were being fulfilled. There was a lessening interest in the affairs of the school together with a less watchful eye on its financial stability by the Trustees. In the second half of the 18th century the school's records are less enlightening.

Whereas it would have been ideal to relate what life was like for the boys in the latter part of the century, from the records available, we can only glean more administrative matters.

On the retirement of Robert Clarke, who had been in charge of both Blue and Grey Coat Schools, a major change took place in that a Mr Tupper was appointed as master of the non-residential Grey Coat school. With this appointment we may expect to see the first signs of a drawing apart of the two boys' charity schools in Chichester. However, as late as 1763 references continue to show a physical union of the two schools. As far as the Grey Coat school was concerned, its income was derived, conventionally, from three main sources: money collected at the infrequent celebrations of the Holy Communion; money collected when the Charity Sermon was preached, and money subscribed by local clergy, headed by the Lord Bishop of Chichester, and local gentry headed by the Duke of Richmond and Gordon. If indeed Whitby's and the Grey Coat school's classrooms were housed under the same roof, this could account for the fact that throughout the first hundred years of the school's existence only two entries in the Grey Coat school accounts are of a material nature—namely, in 1726 a box with lock and handles for the boy's books 8s. 0d. and 'a gang board for the Boys to go up to the forms' in 1731 which cost just 1s. 4d. There is no note of rent paid or money spent on maintaining property. Conversely, Whitby's accounts continue to show considerable expenditure on property.

With reference to the intention and practice of apprenticing, whereas there is a regularity of such fees and payment of leaving bursaries in the Grey Coat accounts, there is a singular lack of apprentice fees in the Whitby accounts. We can only ask ourselves, were those seemingly of the Whitby Foundation financed in this respect from the true 'charity' fund? But without nominal rolls of each school the point can only be one of conjecture.

Between the years 1741 and 1758 the Oliver Whitby accounts actually show debit balances ranging from £4 5s. 1d. to £72 4s. 3¼d. Henry 'Mercer' Peckham, who was at the time acting as cashier to the Trustees, carried the debts personally, paying himself an interest at four and a half per cent. The accounts for these years do not record extraordinary expenditure of any kind nor does the income, derived mainly from the lands at West Wittering, show any decrease, remaining as it did at an average of £200 per annum. Perhaps the cost of living was rising with a lack of proportional increase in the rents of the tenants at Wittering to offset it.

In the middle years of the 18th century the new houses of the gentry began to give a new elegance to the main streets of Chichester, built as they were in warm red brick with what, at the time, were new-fangled sash-windows. The Bishop's Palace was re-faced at the same time and 'a subscription [was] opened for the building of a new Ball Room contiguous to the Council House.' The 'common people' had little to console them, for the summers were bad and they were smitten with 'fevers'. Such was the lot of the poor that the Duke of Richmond ordered his steward to distribute 200lb. of bread 'at 8d. per week till Lady Day next when wheat will be much cheaper'. Entries in the Whitby accounts show Mr Killwick, the Master, being paid 'a free gift' of £5. In the light of subsequent entries, for example, 'to Mr Killwick for his late usual Present from the Trustees at Xmas towards ye Dearness of Provision respecting ye Charity Boys Board, £10 10s.', it is not unreasonable to suppose that the first 'free gift' was, in fact, to offset the high price of victuals.

However, if the poor of the City were being helped directly by the gifts of the nobility and indirectly through Whitby's benefaction and subscriptions in support of the Grey Coat

School, the Mayor, Aldermen and Councillors continued their practice of dining in great state upon Mayor-making day and made, by doing so, such inroads upon the City's finance that they finally had to sell the City Plate in order to remain solvent. On one such occasion an omen of future hostility between the Trustees of Whitby's School and the City appears, for Sir John Miller, M.P. for Chichester and Trustee, declined to attend the Mayor-making and the dinner which followed.

Within the school, the boys were being introduced to an additional subject to their curriculum, for the accounts record the employment of a Mr Burnett to teach the boys to sing, for which he received the sum of £1 1s. 0d. Killwick officially took charge of the Grey Coat school, for which he was to receive £17 0s. 0d. for teaching 20 boys. No mention is made of what may have happened to Mr Tupper. There is an interesting note 'of Mr. Killwick receiving for a Quadrant which he sold as being useless 10/-'. Does this suggest that mathematics was no longer being taught to Whitby boys?

After the slightly precarious financial position of the school noted earlier, matters in 1767 had improved considerably and the Trustees, having paid all their bills and a 'Malish Tax' (Militia?), purchased '£200 Capital Stock in the 4 per cent Consols'. This was the beginning of the gradual invested capital wealth of the school.

Expenditure on behalf of the school records little that is unusual; bills for books and stationery showing minimum spent in 1777 of £1 19s. 0d. and a maximum of £6 8s. 11d. in 1786. The Cathedral pew rent was further reduced to 4s. 0d., sums of money were spent on maintaining the chancel of West Wittering church, more stock was bought, and again the boys were inoculated against the small pox. Maintaining the good health of the boys was not inexpensive—inoculation of the boys cost 10s. 6d.—whilst at the same time a medical practitioner received for his services, in respect of the boys for medicines and attendance, £23 12s. 3d. in one year.

In 1778 Ishmael Killwick is replaced as Master of the Grey Coat School by one Mr Ingram, but remains in charge of Oliver Whitby's until 1792 when the Trustees elect as Master, James McDonald from the parish of Portsea.

As mentioned earlier, one of the popular sights of London had been, and still was up to the end of the 18th century, the public appearances of the Charity Children, when they paraded to special services when sermons were preached and collections taken to swell the funds. As far as Chichester was concerned, although we know that sermons were preached and the Whitby boys paraded and attended church regularly, there was no evidence until 1779 of a special Charity Service being held. However, in this and subsequent years, the accounts record expenditure on 'printing the Anthem 400 leaves', also the printing of the notice of the day the Charity Sermon was to be preached. The origin of this 'Anthem' remains unknown but as time passed it became known as 'The Founders Hymn'. It has continued to be proudly sung not only throughout the life of the school, but also since the school's closure at meetings of Old Oliver Whitbyians.

THE FOUNDER'S HYMN

Our hearts and voices we would raise
In gratitude O Lord to Thee.
Accept our artless song of praise,
And let us all Thy children be.

Sweet charity, the bond of peace,
Inspired our Founder's noble soul.
O may the virtue still increase,
And all our acts and thoughts control.

O may our future conduct show
Instruction has not been in vain;
Do Thou Thy saving grace bestow,
And make our path of duty plain.

The task Thy wisdom hath assigned,
O let us cheerfully fulfil,
In all our works Thy presence find,
And gladly do Thy Holy Will.
Hallelujah! Hallelujah! Hallelujah! Amen.

From 1780 to the end of the century the Charity School movement, as such, declined and lost its initial impetus and educational historians begin to trace the influence of the Sunday School movement. In Chichester the pattern of the times is reflected in the diminishing income of the Grey Coat School. For example, the credit balance in 1788 was but £32 6s. 11d. In contrast the Trustees of Oliver Whitby's School were able to show that financially they were riding on the crest of a wave, with credit balances of £315 2s. 10d., £333 6s. 6¼d. and £593 8s. 5¼d. in the last years of the century. This apparent financial health was to prove in its time a false security but, for the present, the Trustees were content with themselves and the management of the school. Now they even saw fit to pay apprentice indentures, a practice they had not been shown to favour during early years. For example, a premium of £8 8s. was paid to a Joseph Parnell who left the school as apprentice to John Parnell, blacksmith at Harting. The century closed with Whitby's school still confining its attention to only 12 boys, now under a new master, Mr Hackman, who replaced McDonald in 1797.

Though nothing remains to indicate radical changes to the curriculum, it is not possible to confirm or deny that the special provision of the school to teach the rudiments of navigation was being practised. It is, nevertheless, interesting that the accounts record the apprenticing of 'Wm. Smith and Thomas Gardener two of the boys to fit them for Sea Service, £10 8s. 10d.' These were also years of considerable naval activity, with the French Revolution and Napoleonic Wars making the headlines of the day.

The dawn of the 19th century saw the country, in a sense, take a leap forward. These were the times when human and animal power were replaced or supplemented by machines and inanimate power. It was the main age of canal building, the cities were no longer isolated, coach travel was becoming far more frequent and luxurious. But for Oliver Whitby's school, between the years 1800-33, its history was in no way remarkable. The Trustees met only very occasionally; after 21 January 1801 until 4 November 1812 there were only three meetings of the Trustees to pass the accounts, although the large sum of £1,400 was handled over the period. Another Master came and went—Mr Hackman was replaced by Mr Wheatley in 1808 and he, in turn, was replaced by Mr Henry Pescod in 1810.

Oliver Whitby's school continued to plough its lonely furrow, providing education for an extremely limited number of pupils despite an income some ten times what it was initially. In the meantime, the Grey Coat School for boys staggered on with its sister Blue Coat Girls School, despite ever decreasing subscriptions. But also at this time new, and in a sense, rival forces were at work at the national level which were to make an impact on Chichester and to provide the Whitby boys with new neighbours. Ultimately, by the 20th century, there were educational facilities in the face of which an unmodified Charity School, even of the highest grade, could not survive. This outside influence came in the form of schools founded according to the principles of Dr Andrew Bell and Joseph Lancaster.

The education of the poor again became, just as it had a hundred years earlier, the interest of the moment for the fashionable and learned world. The decrease in child mortality together with the growing use of child labour forced the State to look into the question of the provision of education. Yet in the first half of the 19th century the privately financed, semi-publicly administered provision of elementary schooling received a new lease of life which enabled it to impose itself as the voluntary system of national education.

A long and stubborn struggle, fought between the supporters and opponents of State intervention in education, resulted, in 1833, in a compromise which showed the strength of the voluntary principle. Unable both because of religious jealousies to compel the application of the rates to education, and also of the jealousy of vested interests to control endowments for the education of the poor, educational reformers fell back upon the demand for financial assistance from the State. After one such heated debate, with very poor attendance, the Commons, by a majority of 50-26, voted to supply the sum of £20,000 a year for the creation of School Houses.

This, the first parliamentary grant to State education, has acquired an importance as a landmark within the modern education system which is undeserved. The sum set aside for elementary education was small, too small, as Joseph Hume remarked in the House: 'It committed the Government to no policy, and did not increase their responsibilities.' It was merely a recognition by the State of the voluntary system of education.

Like so many successful ideas, new plans for the schoolroom had come about by accident. Teachers employed in an orphan charity school at Madras in India refused to obey the instructions of the superintendent, the Rev. Andrew Bell. The elder boys were called upon to take their place in the school, and carried out their duties so efficiently that Bell wrote a pamphlet telling the public of the success of his new discovery, the mutual system of education.

The Quaker, Joseph Lancaster, master of a school for the poor, in Southwark, developed the idea. Lancaster's benevolence, his enthusiasm, his remarkable powers as organiser and teacher, together with the rewards and punishments which he devised, attracted vast numbers of children. But as the cost of each child's instruction worked out at a guinea a year, and with subscriptions minimal, he could only admit a limited number of charity children. However, the 'Mutual or Monitorial System' solved his problem. 'It demonstrated that seven children could be educated for a guinea instead of one'. Success bred success, subscriptions poured in and, with the money factor eliminated, his charity school was financed on the same lines as the old Charity Schools, the point where, in Lancaster's enormous school of 1,000 children in the Borough Road, the whole system of tuition was almost entirely conducted by the boys. There is no doubt that the success of the Bell and Lancaster concept gave new impetus to the moribund system of the Charity Schools and expanded voluntary effort to embrace, more than supplement, the inadequacies of the Sunday School. This invigoration of an old system is nowhere more clearly demonstrated than in Chichester.

In the early autumn citizens had invited Lancaster to Chichester to address a public meeting in the Assembly Room. He accepted the invitation and, on 13 September 1810, a Society was formed 'for the Education of the Poor of Chichester and its Environs on the Plan of Joseph Lancaster'. Lancaster promised to provide a schoolmaster and subscribers guaranteed £1 1s. 0d. per annum to the Society. So the Lancastrian school was born and the subsequent months were occupied in acquiring further subscribers and making rules concerning the children to be admitted. Of all the clauses, that concerning their religious exercise is perhaps the most interesting in the light of subsequent criticism. On Sundays all children had to attend church or their respective meeting houses and to return to school to be instructed in the catechism. However, in Chichester a partisan spirit may have prevailed for, in November 1811, when the school had been in operation but 10 months, the Committee of the Society printed leaflets for general distribution in which it was made more than clear that the principles and doctrines of the Church of England were to be the sole basis of all teaching and instruction. in the school.

Thus, the residential element apart, there was to be little difference between this 'new' school and its well entrenched predecessor. In fact, the similarities are even more striking. As Whitby's Trustees had set up their box and Blue Boy for passing charity and, by doing so, conformed to a national pattern, so now the Committee of the Lancastrian school set up 'an occasional money box' in their porch in the hope of supplementing their subscribed income. So that the good folk of the City might not have the opportunity to suspect what went on behind closed doors, Whitby Trustees had arranged for their boys to be publicly examined, so likewise the Lancastrian invited inspection by the public 'on Mondays, Wednesdays and Fridays between 11 and 12'.

The Lancastrian school had no rival, for the Oliver Whitby school was markedly different, if only because of its residential nature. The two Charity Schools, Grey Coat Boys and Blue Coat Girls, were scarcely surviving with some two dozen children and an income of less than £50 per annum. However, at the end of 1811, the clergy of the diocese met at the instigation of the Bishop, and set up 'The Sussex Society for the Education of the Infant Poor in the Principles of the Established Church'. Endless meetings were held during which the Committee decided that new schools should be called The Sussex Central Schools. They also decided on a site for a boys' school immediately outside the East Wall, but the City Council declined to breach the City wall to allow access to the new school site. So pious plans were thwarted until the middle of 1812 when the Committee included among its members three prominent laymen knowledgeable of the practical aspects of running a school. These men were Peachey, Woods and Brereton, three senior Trustees of the Whitby Foundation. On 2 November 1812 the 'Central' boys' school was opened on a new site in New Park Road in a building erected for the sum of £600, and in the charge of Mr James Baker at a salary of £75 per annum. At the same time the affairs of the Grey Coat Boys' and the Blue Coat Girls' Schools were wound up.

Lest the Committee be regarded as intolerant of Dissent the Trustees declared that 'the advantages arising from their Institution be refused to no children on account of their Parents being Dissenters from the Church of England'. There was, however, a sting in the tail for, they continued, the children were to be without exception instructed in the liturgy and catechism of the established church.

Another little difficulty arose in that Headmaster Green's interest in the Lancastrian school lessened since he was receiving but two third's of his 'rival's' salary and Mr Pescod, at Whitby's School, was housed and fed and paid in return for teaching but 12 boys almost £50 per quarter. So suddenly and discreetly off to London went James Florance, the City Surveyor, to meet Lancaster and explain the position and ask for a replacement teacher, 'more competent than Green'. Green was peremptorily sacked and given 'a present of £10'. His successor, Mr Bosworth, gave even less satisfaction to the Committee for they soon noted in their minutes 'a falling off in credit of the school' and were concerned at the brutal corporal punishment that Bosworth meted out.

This unhappy state of affairs was, no doubt, much to the liking of the Committee of the Central School who prided themselves upon their good judgement in selecting Baker as the Master. The problem of maintaining attendance at the Lancastrian school was still proving difficult. Bosworth, like Green, was sacked, a Mr Paull was appointed, sent on a course at Godalming and, despite the Committee's earlier aversion to corporal punishment, they saw fit to authorise the procuring of a 'rod' and the installation of 'a pair of stocks in the classroom'.

Oliver Whitby Trustees had little to occupy themselves with during this period of significant upheaval in local education, with the arrival of two schools which some may have thought as competitive elements. They allocated money for the re-building of their farm buildings at Wittering, painted the outside of their House in West Street and negotiated the purchase of some £3,000 of Capital Stock. They were, however, as has been demonstrated, active on behalf of the National Society and saw fit to divert £100 of their capital towards the building of a new National School at Birdham, also voting a sum of £5 per annum towards its maintenance. This action was subsequently questioned by the Commissioners on the 'Education of the Poor.

At the national level, numerous reports were submitted to Parliament making it clear that there was a desire, if not a demand, of the 'lower orders' for education. The main problem was that of finance. However, in 1816 Henry Peter Brougham M.P. persuaded Parliament to appoint a Select Committee on the Education of the Lower Orders and pressed for an investigation into the use of educational charities. Two years later Brougham obtained an act appointing Commissioners to enquire into them. During the course of their investigation the Commissioners visited Chichester and reported on what they found or rather what they were told. Whilst incumbents of the City parishes testified to a man that the poor had 'ample means of education' or 'sufficient means of education' available at 'the national schools', only one voice, that of the Rev. Tuffnell, Vicar of St Bartholomew's, bothered to mention 'some other school'. But in 1819 the Commissioners took full evidence from the Trustees of the Whitby School and recorded their findings in detail. It would appear they were duly impressed by the details provided for them by the Trustees, and recorded that the boys 'are instructed in reading, writing, arithmetic, mathematics and the rudiments of navigation'. As already noted, it is questionable as to whether they were in fact instructed in navigation and there is no way of telling. The Commissioners were concerned with finance and probably never went near the school to see for themselves. It would have been boorish to have done so when they had received the hospitality of the Trustees at the *Dolphin* or the *Swan*, at a cost of £2 15s. 0d.

Brougham was able to demonstrate the total inadequacy of educational provision at the national level—a state of affairs that owed its comparative improvement only to the efforts of Bell and Lancaster. Their schools had made provision nationally for about 200,000 children since there inception in 1803. However, despite all the evidence, Brougham's Bill of 1820 came to nothing and in Chichester, at least, the 'rival' schools continued whilst Oliver Whitby's 12 boys remained immured in West Street, apart from a spell of six months that they spent in 'a House in the Cathedrall Church Yard' when £442 13s. 10d. was spent by the Trustees in 'rebuilding' the school house. Though the accounts for the early 1820s show little except domestic items such as the cleaning of Whitby's memorial in the cloisters and the occasional apprenticing 'to sea service', the Trustees, inspired perhaps by the earnestness of the Commissioners who had visited them, and mindful of the principles behind their inquiry, began the necessary legal proceedings to enable them to extend the benefits of the Charity they administered. This they were able to do by an order of the Master of the Rolls dated 25 May 1826. By this order they were empowered to increase the number of boys to twenty and subsequently, at their discretion, as the financial state of the Charity permitted. They were also given authority to employ an Assistant Master.

The number of boys was increased and additional bedding, furniture, horn mugs, pewter plates and silver badges, now supplied from London, were bought. The Trustees also benefited the little girls of the Central School, by employing them to make new sheets and shirts for the additional boys at the Whitby School. Despite a total expenditure for 1826 of £1,217 5s. 9¼d. the Trustees still had a credit balance at the end of the year of £1,160 19s. 2¾d.—no small sum for this time.

Whilst all continued well with Oliver Whitby's School, both the Lancastrian and Central Schools were feeling a financial strain and were hard put to survive. Mr Paull (Junior) continued as master of the Lancastrian, but now Mr Baker at the Central suddenly proved 'unsatisfactory' and even a reduction in his salary failed to make him mend his ways and he was summarily dismissed. However, the ladies connected with the Central Schools organised a bazaar to be held in the Assembly Room after Easter. According to the *Hampshire Telegraph*, this was a most elegant affair and, perhaps because of the choice articles that were for sale or because of the charm of the ladies, the schools benefited by £350. With fees of 2d. per week for boys and 1d. per week for girls, together with collections from Charity Sermons, suddenly financial security seemed assured.

After the Charity Sermon preached in the Cathedral on 14 May 1832, and no doubt listened to by the boys of the Whitby School who now numbered 28 and sat on their newly painted stools since the Trustees had declined to pay pew rent since 1822, the *Hampshire Telegraph* reports, 'Children of the Central Schools, 370 in number including Blue Girls and Grey Coat Boys were regaled with 200lbs. of plum duff and beer' and 'returned in procession displaying banners and huzzaing with all their might'.

But if the Oliver Whitby Boys were deprived of material succour on 14 May, they were to have their turn during the celebrations of the Reform Bill in June. The *Hampshire Telegraph* tells us that on 16 June the shops closed at 12 o'clock midday and after a great procession through the streets, in which the children took part, there was a great fair in the Sloe-Fair Field outside Northgate. In the evening, the Market Cross was lit by candies and the City at large enjoyed a display of fireworks whilst the 'gentry' partook of a banquet in the Assembly Room. Although no mention is made of the Lancastrian children at these events, they had their own treat by visiting Kingley Vale, a wooded valley some five miles from Chichester, surrounded by hills on which are ancient British burial grounds locally called 'The Devil's Humps'.

During the remaining months of 1832 cholera raged throughout summer and the Trustees of Whitby's School wisely spent money 'repairing and emptying the privies'. Paganini played in the Assembly Room on 8 September and Sir Walter Scott, whose books would adorn the shelves of all schools in future years, died on 21 September.

Whereas the early part of the century was not a remarkable period in the history of the Oliver Whitby School, during the period 1833-70 there were considerable developments within education as a whole which had significance as far as the School was concerned. At the national level 1833 saw the beginning of state intervention in education. There was also a changed situation in Chichester with regard to the provision of general education in as much that the Central School and Lancastrian School were well established and there were now nine 'private schools' as well. Thus the total number of children attending schools was 727 in the Central and Lancastrian Schools and also 357 in the 'private schools' which included Oliver Whitby's and the Cathedral Prebendal School. This total of 1,084 represented some 10 per cent of the total population of the City, barely 9,000 at this time.

Nonconformist and church relations were hardening at this time as a result of the Oxford Movement. Prominent in Chichester was Archdeacon Manning, a powerful figure in the movement. He preached strongly the Church's right to educate, and, likewise, a hardening attitude towards 'sabbath breakers' and the 'evasion' of Sunday School is reflected in the minutes of the Central Schools under his Chairmanship. This whole question of religious or rather denominational teaching was to prove a difficulty for many years to come. Briefly, the dispute was that if money voted by Parliament was to be used for school buildings of any kind, the Church for its part argued that it could not and would not support a scheme that made no provision for denominational teaching. Conversely, and understandably seen through modern eyes, the Dissenters would not bring themselves to contribute, through rates or taxes, for doctrinal teaching in schools.

Tension was not eased when the Committee of Council, whose duty it was to determine how grants of money were to be distributed, decided that future distribution of money would rest upon the result of inspection. In Chichester it took several years for the results of this directive to be seen or felt. Oliver Whitby's School was too independent, historically and by inclination, to be concerned with grants or inspections nor was it within the category of schools to which the Minute referred. The Trustees of the school did their best to alleviate the financial difficulties of the National Society locally by making annual donations of £25 each to their schools in the vicinity of Chichester, including Harting, and by purchasing school books from the Diocesan Committee and continuing 'employing' the Girls' School to make sheets and shirts for the boys! Whilst these sums donated were a substantial part of the National Schools income, the amount in any one year was, by contrast, only about one per cent of the Whitby's School's income. The Trustees did, however, undertake the building of a new school in West Wittering in 1849. This school building can still be seen as it has been reconstructed within the Weald and Downland Open Air Museum at Singleton, near Chichester. It appears to have been a conversion rather than a new building: it is now thought to have been an open-ended cartshed, possibly dating from the 18th century. The open end was filled in and gables were added to the roof, interior walls were plastered, the floor paved with stone slabs and a chimney was provided for a stove. In the yard outside, there is evidence of other lean-to buildings one of which was a stable, possibly for the schoolmistress's horse. Within the building at the museum are preserved many items of the school's furniture together with such articles as might well have been used for teaching both at Wittering and at Oliver Whitby's in Chichester.

The Church, at the centre, whilst all this charitable work proceeded, spent its customary months deliberating 'the expediency of putting the schools under Government inspection'. Eventually, but not until 1847, it was resolved to press 'for early inspection'.

During the next decade Whitby Trustees bought a neighbouring property in Tower Street at a cost of £270 0s. 0d. to accommodate their increased numbers of 38 boys by the end of 1852, and also bought a garden behind the school 'to be used as a Play and Exercise Ground'. They started once more the practice of awarding premiums to the boys who left and employed an official cashier at a salary of £20 per annum. In the little world of Chichester itself, life pursued its customary path. Archdeacon Manning continued to be the object of the bitterest attacks, even though he had been received into the Church of Rome in April 1851.

But two matters began to occupy the correspondence columns of the *Hampshire Telegraph* and also the *West Sussex Gazette* which ultimately were to become cardinal factors affecting the destiny and fate of Oliver Whitby's School. Unbelievable as it may seem these were, firstly, the state of the Cathedral School and, secondly, the lack of sanitation in the City. Although the specific problems were not the direct concern of the Trustees and neither would be resolved quickly, the argument was that Chichester needed drains and that the Cathedral School appeared moribund, St Mary's Hospital was wealthy and supported but a handful of old ladies; and Whitby's School funds were likewise in a good state and only being used by/ for limited application. Thus ideas began to take shape for a wider use of these financial resources that would benefit the community at large. As we shall see, this debate would continue for some time.

Meanwhile, the Whitby boys saw the old houses opposite the school pulled down and the north side of the Cathedral opened up to view. Also they acquired a new neighbour: a new church, St Peter the Great commonly called 'the sub-deanery', was built on the corner

4 The interior of the West Wittering school, financed and run by the Oliver Whitby Trust and possibly dating from the 18th century. Many of the items displayed would have been very similar to those used at the Blue Coat School in Chichester during the Victorian period.

of West Street and Tower Street. (This church replaced the parochial activity in the Cathedral's north transept.) Perhaps too the fall of decaying masonry from the roof of the north transept which caused the boys to be hurried from the Cathedral in 1853 presaged what was to happen to the spire not many years later.

Academically, the School's curriculum at the time appears to have been similar to that offered by the Central School and its rival, the Lancastrian. The timetable included:

Catechism and Liturgy with Scripture Proofs
Ciphering (New Rules)
Writing upon paper
Arithmetic (Old Rules)
Reading New Testament
Linear Drawing
Writing from Dictation or Memory
Ciphering (Old Rules)
Outlines of Geography
History
Vocal Music

Even if the comparative calm of the city had little to trouble it after 39 years of peace, in the early months of 1854 war in the Crimea was declared and on 4 May the Whitby Boys attended a special service on the day of the National Fast. However, despite the war the boys attended, at half price, a performance of 'Hoffman's Organophonic Band' in the Assembly Room and also a performance of 'Macartes Monster American Circus', whilst free entertainment came in the form of manoeuvres of the militia outside the School House 'in order to induce recruitment'.

When Sebastopol fell there was music through the streets, 'banners floated and the bells pealed'. Local efforts were made to alleviate the distress caused by the high cost of provisions by running a soup kitchen at the *Dolphin Hotel*, a few doors away from the school.

However, peace returned to the Country and while Whitby Boys played cricket, football and all manner of sport. In the capital city Charles Dickens was bringing home to his readers, with devastating clarity, the injustices of Victorian England, making them aware of the need for better education facilities and for the replacement of overcrowded slums by decent housing with proper sanitary arrangements. Chichester in 1857 was itself turning its attention to these important matters—adult or further education and, not least, drains! So—whilst the City promoted the setting up of a night-school, in which it was supported by the *West Sussex Gazette* with some doggerel verse:

Come from the Pancras, and come from the Broyle,
Men of the anvil and sons of the soil,
Come to be taught to read, Writing come learn it.
Stout lords of Summer Town, men of the Hornet,

Put up your 'bacco pipes—leave the beer houses;
Spend no more money on nightly carouses;
Lounge not at market cross—be like your betters;
Come learn to read—write all your own letters—come to night school.

—the vexed matter of 'the drains' remained a contentious issue. Meanwhile an anonymous donor made an intriguing gift to the Oliver Whitby School in the form of a celestial globe mounted on a stand with compass attached. This may have indicated that a certain amount of mathematics, in relation to navigation, was still being taught. In any case Pescod, the Master, was 'Curator of Apparatus' to the Mechanics Institute in the City, and this may be a clue as to the globe's acquisition by the school.

The winter of 1860–61 was very severe and snow lay deep for a long time in the streets of the City. The Whitby boys were sick and had special attention throughout these winter months. But their sickness was of little importance in comparison with that of the Cathedral fabric, revealed by the removal of the Arundel Screen in July 1859. The great pillars of the spire were discovered to be filled with no more than rubble and so, because of the imminent danger of the fall of the spire, the Cathedral was closed. The boys went to the new Subdeanery Church of St Peter the Great on Sundays for their customary services. One can imagine their excitement as they watched from the school windows opposite the shoring up of the spire and learnt of the evacuation of the nearby houses, wondering if they might get a reprieve from their regimented routine. Despite all efforts to save it the spire fell on 21 February 1861 at approximately 1.30 p.m., not toppling over as many had feared, but 'as one telescope tube slides into another, the mass of the tower crumbled beneath it'.

Spring finally came to lift Chichester from its darkest winter. Cathedral services had been transferred to St Andrew's Church. The Lancastrian schools celebrated their jubilee on 7 March with 36 gallons of tea and 400 lbs of plum-cake. But the fall of the spire occupied the correspondence columns of all papers both at national and local level with everything and everyone being blamed. Even the Queen commanded that she be sent 'stereoscopic views of the ruins'.

In summer 1861 the Whitby boys made an important public appearance at the launching of the new Selsey Lifeboat in the Canal Basin at Chichester. 'At the special request of Captain Pilkington the boys of the Oliver Whitby School (Blue Coat Boys) whose studies are especially directed to navigation, were present during the whole ceremony.' It is doubtful if navigation, whatever its precise meaning, was being taught at this time.

The summer saw the boys making their annual visit to Kingley Vale and also playing cricket on their newly rented cricket field. The school accounts show that the Trustees spent £7 5s. 3d. on rubble from the fallen spire which was used to fill in the cellar of one of their recently acquired houses in Tower Street. A School of Art was opened in Chichester attached to the Mechanics Institute, the Central Schools were reported to be in debt and the year ended with the sudden death of the Prince Consort on 14 December.

The Newcastle Commission, charged 'to inquire into the present state of education in England, and to consider and report what measures, if any, are required for the extension of sound and cheap elementary instruction to all classes of people', issued its report in 1861. The commission had taken note of the litte local difficulty in Chichester in maintaining attendance and the expedients varying from punishment to pudding and plum cake that the Lancastrian and Central Schools devised to combat the apparent zeal of some to avoid education, even when a pittance was being paid by hard-pressed parents. This question of attendance occupied the minds of the Commissioners at the national level and a complicated system of grants was drawn up. Another factor was the tendency of up to three-quarters of those children who went to school to leave at the age of ten or before they were eleven. Here there emerges a clear picture as to the status of the Oliver Whitby School academically *vis à vis* the Central and Lancastrian schools. Irrespective of the material benefits to be derived from the Charity, it is clear from the admission registers that pupils were admitted from both these schools in order to benefit, presumably, from the higher education at the time. Even as early as 1826 Oliver Whitby's had been looked upon as a reward for 'intelligence and good conduct' with some of these pupils staying as they did until at least the age of fourteen.

In 1860 a national Code had been formed which made it clear that government grants to schools were dependent upon, at least, a daily reading of the Scriptures and being open to Her Majesty's Inspectors. This system of examination affected in a small way the Oliver Whitby School. Though quite independent of state aid, the idea of a yearly examination and report appealed to the Trustees, so, on 1 January 1863, the Principal of the Chichester Theological College examined the boys of the school. The *West Sussex Gazette* pronounced the Whitby Foundation 'one of the best managed Charities in the Kingdom'. In this same year the Prince of Wales was married and 'The Blue Coat Boys' appeared before the public and 'had a glorious dinner of roast beef, plum pudding and cake provided by the Trustees in the evening'. The *West Sussex Gazette* reported that the boys drank enthusiastically the health of the Queen, and the Prince of Wales!

In 1865 cholera raged in the City as it had done regularly since the first epidemic in 1831. The Trustees paid a doctor's bill of £37 14s. 6d. for inoculation, which must have been successful as we have no record of any boys succumbing to the disease. Once more the campaign for drainage and the removal of the cattle markets from the streets became the subject of the day. The following year, 1866, saw the completion of the new spire with celebrations held on 28 June and Oliver Whitby Boys taking part in a grand procession. As one can imagine, the day was spent merry-making with public dinners and fireworks in the evening. According to the Whitby accounts the Trustees had been pleased to donate £100 towards the restoration of the Cathedral 'because of the free sittings of the boys for upward of 150 years'. Either the cashier had not looked back in the accounts to see that a rent had originally been paid or this donation was for the 'reserved space' which the boys always enjoyed, even up to the time of the school's closure.

Sadly, the merry-making in June was marred by yet more cholera, and the local press was full of attacks on the City Council for failing to take bold steps. The Secretary of State was advised of the conditions of the City. Active among the campaigners for some scheme of main drainage was Dr Tyacke, member of the Council, but he with a fellow councillor, Freeland, received his 'reward' at the November elections when they both came bottom of the poll. The electorate were terrified by the proposed cost of a drainage scheme and preferred to believe Dr Bostock who claimed that 'water from cesspools dug to a depth of nine foot when drained into wells whose average depth is nineteen feet is far purer than water carried through pipes from wells at Fishbourne'. The City divided into the 'Drainers' and the 'Non-Drainers' as they remained known for many years. Dr Tyacke was a Dissenter, manager of the Lancastrian school and a Drainer. Dr Bostock was Church, Cathedral supported and a Non-Drainer. So fierce was the local battle that it drew national interest, with people such as John Stuart Mill, the great political thinker of the age, becoming involved in correspondence in the *West Sussex Gazette*, on the side of the Drainers.

While concern over the provision of elementary education had grown during the 1850-60s there had been similar concern about secondary education. These years saw the rise of many proprietary schools, both boarding and day, of which Radley, Ardingly and the City of London School are typical, whilst in Chichester the Middle School provided 'education for young gentlemen of 7 to 14 years of age at 50 Guineas a Term for Boarders'. The Whitby School, it could be argued, now occupied this sort of position for (as we have seen earlier) boys were transferred from the Grey Coat Boys and Central elementary schools, and other boys, hardly to be called poor since they were the sons of prominent business men or even of the Trustees themselves, attended and availed themselves of the Charity. But of course there was still no place for Dissenters. However, it should be added that in general the terms of the Charity were not abused.

The Government in 1864 appointed a Royal Commission, under the chairmanship of Lord Taunton, to enquire into the education given in schools not included in an earlier Public Schools Commission 'and to consider and report what measures (if any) are required for the improvement of such education, having especial regard to all endowments applicable or which can rightly be made applicable thereto'. The report published in 1868 demonstrated the woeful inadequacy of secondary education. The report revealed that almost half of a total of 782 old endowed schools not only did not give instruction in Greek or Latin but also seldom gave any effective instruction in mathematics, French or natural science. In reality they 'gave an education no wider than that of an ordinary elementary school'.

Naturally enough Oliver Whitby's School was a legitimate object for the attention of the Commissioners. But again the Trustees chose to pursue their policy of exclusiveness, and why not indeed? They had plenty of money, they elected to their own body of Trustees by whim apart from acknowledging their Founder's clause requiring membership of the Church of England, they saw to it that no Dissenter darkened their door, and would have no truck with the City Council! However, a Commissioner, H.A. Giffard, visited Chichester in the early part of 1867 and reported that the School had 'been assumed by the Trustees to be beyond the range of this Commission, and no information has been furnished in answer to the printed schedules of inquiry which were sent to them'. The Trustees showed little interest and, rather than entertain the commissioner as their predecessors had done in 1819, the accounts only record a lavish annual audit dinner at £11 3s. 5d. together with the payment for a silver watch (with an inscription therein) given to a Charles Hanmore. This was a reward for saving the lives of two boys, Guy and Rawlins, from being drowned while bathing at the Apuldram Sluice—where the Lavant joins Chichester Harbour. Giffard, however, did manage to obtain some of the information he required, giving a fair picture of the school at that time.

He assessed the school as 'non-classical' and of the 'third grade', emphasising the essentially unchanged nature of the school since its foundation. At that time (1867) the school now had a total of 46 boys. All studied arithmetic, geography, reading, writing, drawing (including geometric drawing and freehand) and they all also received religious instruction. Twenty-four boys studied history, English grammar and English composition: twenty-two did physics: twenty, mathematics and mensuration with another 12 also spending time on book-keeping.

It was clear to the commissioner that the course of study was 'modified in the case of scholars who showed aptitude, who are intended for certain lines of life, and who are disqualified for certain parts of School work'. Here was a small residential school whose boys were admitted according to merit, where corporal punishment was rare and carried out by the headmaster only and where discipline in the dormitories was maintained by senior boys.

Clearly Giffard found himself at a loss and records, in somewhat pathetic tones: 'I have been unable to ascertain to what extent the instruction prescribed by the founder is carried out. But the direction to teach the mathematics is *prima facie* evidence that he did not intend the boys, whether they were the sons of labourers or not, to be tied down to the position of labourers.' He continues: 'I do not know under the circumstances how far it is within my province to make recommendations concerning the school. But if it should be thought to be within the scope of the Inquiry, then it might (supposing such a course to be thought expedient) admit of annexation or subordination to the Prebendal school which is in close proximity to it.' Obviously Mr Giffard did not raise this idea whilst in the presence of the hyper-sensitive Trustees or he would soon have learned of the many reasons, most stemming from petty pride and jealousies, why this course of action would have been intolerable to them. They were proud inheritors and trustees of a flourishing and successful school and across the road there was a school which, at this time, was barely functioning. For the Whitby Trustees the Prebendal School had all the signs of clerical incompetence and *laissez-faire*, factors that had involved their predecessors in action, as opposed to talk, at the time of the setting up of the National Society schools in the City. The prospect of annexation or subordination would have been unthinkable. Much more acceptable would have been the idea that the Oliver Whitby Trustees might administer the Prebendal School.

Thus the school remained with Mr Pescod as Master and an active young assistant, Mr Ballard, whose family was prominent in the City. The findings of the Commission aroused considerable interest but resulted in little practical outcome. The various abortive projects, resolutions and bills to improve the education scene were finally brought to a head in 1870. A Bill reached the statute book, the chief concern of which was the provision of efficient schools throughout the country in places where none existed. The Bill included a Conscience Clause which gave a right to exemption from religious instruction. Another clause made attendance for the ages of five to 13 obligatory.

Four

Headmaster Ballard: The 'Drains' and Prior's Scheme 1871–1904

The introduction of the Elementary Education Act of 1870, which the state initiated for the provision of primary education instead of providing financial help to the voluntary bodies, did not have an obvious effect in Chichester. The Central and Lancastrian schools continued to flourish, while Oliver Whitby's provided a 'higher' level of education. The school at this time was, without doubt, very efficient, financially stable and above all fulfilled the intentions of its founder. At the national level, schools such as Westminster Grey Coat School, Liverpool Blue Coat School and Christ's Hospital itself were adapting themselves to changing educational demands and opportunities, but Oliver Whitby's School, through the obstinacies and lack of vision of its Trustees, was entering a period during which it risked becoming an educational backwater.

The tide was about to change and the old order would be swept away forever. In 1870 Mr Pescod's health was failing. Master for 29 years, he was advised, according to a curt and impersonal minute of the Trustees in June 1871, 'that he should entirely abstain from taking any part either in the Education or discipline of the school until he learn further from the Trustees'. During the period of the headmaster's failing health, Mr C.H.R. Ballard, who had served as assistant master in the school since 1864, had been scrupulous in keeping the Trustees informed of the conduct and behaviour of the boys, in conducting examinations, and seeing that the boys were all vaccinated 'according to orders'. In July 1871 the Trustees appointed Mr Ballard master at a salary of £120 per annum with board and lodgings. Mr Pescod was dismissed and, in recognition of many years' service, the Trustees awarded a pension of £25 per year, also agreeing to Pescod's request to live in the small house in Tower Street, next to the school, where his sister was presently living. But, within a month and for whatever reason, the Trustees repented of their generosity, repealed their minute by limiting the pension to two years only, and ejected both Pescod and his sister from their house, declining even to allow them to remain

5   Charles R. Ballard: Headmaster 1871 to 1908.

35

6 Probably the first photograph of an Oliver Whitby boy in uniform, believed to have been taken in 1865.

until November of that year. The injustice of the Trustees' action provoked Pescod to write to the Endowed Schools Commission and, his case seemingly justified, they wrote to the Trustees suggesting a pension of £50 per annum. The Trustees ignored the Commissioners' letter; only after a reminder they replied that they were 'not disposed to incur any further responsibility beyond the gratuity of £25 already granted for two years'. After the Commissioners' further correspondence the Trustees asked to be allowed to provide a pension of £20 per annum adding: 'The Trustees in coming to this decision beg to observe that they do not consider that this Charity is bound to provide for its Masters on their retirement and the Trustees consent to do so on the present occasion, only on account of the peculiar circumstances attending this case.' The Commissioners argued that the sum of money, bearing in mind the total income of the school, was little enough, but the final word was with the Trustees who wrote that they were 'unanimously resolved that they would not entertain any further application for an increase'. This domestic squabble reveals again that same high-handed independence that marked the Trustees' attitude to the Schools Enquiry Commission and which was to be their prevailing perspective for the next thirty years.

The years of Mr Ballard as headmaster of the school were to be the most significant years in the school's history. There is no doubt he was an efficient master; with him in command the Trustees need not worry. But he was ruthless and tyrannical, as local legend still recalls and the evidence of Old Boys supports. He held the destinies of the school in his hands during the years of immense educational opportunity in both secondary and higher education. Oliver Whitby School was his empire and this he would defend against all assailants. His personal and public defences proved unassailable, but of vision he had none except for his private good.

With the advent of Ballard much of the administration of the school was changed. Would-be participants in the benefits of the Charity were now required to seek admission in response to advertisements in the local paper, the *West Sussex Gazette*. Candidates currently attending local elementary schools were considered by the Trustees. 'All those who had brothers at the school and others whose parents were able, from their earnings, to educate their own children', were rejected. Boys who were eligible were 'elected after an examination in reading, writing from dictation, the Church Catechism and the simple rules of Arithmetic'. While maintaining the objective of providing places for the poor, before this date the school had been educationally attractive as it provided the best education locally. However, now it was in competition with the day schools whose standard of education was rising. Therefore, Oliver Whitby's now became more philanthropically attractive and sought to nurture generations of grateful poor. However, such charity was dispensed by a domineering and tyrannical master and was provided, at a distance, by a condescending and patronising board of Trustees, who saw themselves as bountiful to the lower classes. They in their turn had the duty to serve, whilst breathing sighs of gratitude in the ears of their patrons. So, no boy was admitted whose conduct was anything but excellent or whose family had fewer than five children in it or an income of more than 25s. per week. Those most commonly accepted for admission came from families of ten, eleven or twelve children, the record being seventeen.

Ballard was ruthless in reporting misdemeanours and in expelling boys who, in his opinion, were idle. The minutes of the Trustees during the first five years of his reign are littered with cases of truancy (running away), and of investigation by the Trustees, of harshness by Ballard. Generally, and understandably, both the boys and their parents, when summoned to appear before the Trustees, failed to do so and they invariably found that 'the master had not been guilty of undue severity'. Ballard had the complete confidence of his employers, and so he should, for he was known around the City for demanding high quality from suppliers of materials for the boys' clothes and the provisions from local contractors. Also, on the positive side, he ensured that the boys were vaccinated at the proper time and that they were confirmed at the discretion of the Trustees. He also arranged a visit to the Crystal Palace as a holiday treat and purchased a harmonium to ensure better musical training. During his early days, gas was introduced into the school for better lighting of the school room, dining room and dormitories. The satisfaction of the Trustees was demonstrated by their increasing his salary from £120 to £170 in the five years from his assuming office.

Financially the school continued to thrive and the number of boys again increased to 50 in 1886 and 52 by 1878, the highest number in the school's history. However, Ballard must have been extremely difficult to work with, for in the course of one year, 1877, he had three assistant masters, Fletcher, Harvey and Green. Neither an addition to their salary of £5 per annum for teaching the boys music nor an allowance of cash in lieu of beer persuaded them to stay.

Typhoid was still a local scourge and, though the school was connected to main water supply in 1878, the cesspits continued to be a source of anxiety. As a result of infection contracted at the school or on a visit to his parents' house to collect his clean linen, one of the boys died. Though the boys were fully clothed and boarded at the school, one of the traditions was that parents were responsible for laundry. It was a familiar sight in the City to see the boys once a week carrying their clothes in a dark blue linen bag. Over the years this tradition changed; the boys remained at school and the parents visited the school to collect laundry and leave clean linen. This change may have been introduced to minimise truancy and absconding which had become serious problems in the 1870s and '80s.

Although at this time Oliver Whitby's was still not subject to visits by Her Majesty's Inspectors, the Trustees continued their own practice of ensuring that the boys were frequently examined and inspected, either by themselves or by a specially appointed examiner. Among those invited to inspect the school was Dr Morris of King's College, author of *Specimens of Early English*. Comments from the reports of the time demonstrate most clearly the status of the school: 'The scholars went through a little elementary drill and performed revolutions very creditably.' 'The boys are receiving a sound elementary education, and one well adapted to the surroundings of the pupils and calculated to promote their usefulness after leaving school.' 'The standard of attainment is considerably above that of the average for boys of the same age in Public Elementary Schools and the thorough and careful character of the work is highly creditable.' The Trustees, for their part, were more concerned with the cleanliness and well-being of the boys and invariably found them to be satisfactory. There was one little matter which gave cause for concern; haircutting had become unacceptable and so Mr Greenfield, the barber, was given 'a quarter's notice as his eyesight was getting too defective for haircutting'.

Mr Ballard had a mania about cleanliness, as old boys of the school have testified. Conditions were spartan and hot water for washing was allowed only once a week. There was no bath at this time, but the boys made use of a foot-bath. Ballard invented a ritual which he described to the Charity Commissioner as follows: 'It has always been my custom to have the boys every few days 'show up' which means that they appear at bed time before me with their shirts wrapped around their waist so that I am able to see their shoulders, chests, knees and feet are clean. Even that is much in advance of the inhabitants generally for there is no public bath in Chichester and only quite recently a water supply.' According to one old boy, even a history textbook which attributed the causes of the Great Plague to 'dirt' was amended by Ballard to read 'stale dirt'.

Following the merger of the Endowed Schools Commission and the Charity Commission, the new body in 1882 turned its attention to the state of Chichester's two major endowed schools, the Prebendal or Cathedral School, and Oliver Whitby's School. The Commissioner saw that, on the one hand, was the Prebendal, whose history could best be described as spasmodic and a traditional grammar school; on the other hand was Whitby's School, wealthy, efficient and flourishing but extremely limited in educational scope and inhibited in the distribution of favours. However, an Anglican foundation was common to the two schools, and the Commissioners sent shock waves through those concerned by their suggestion for the union of the two schools and/or the addition of day scholars to Oliver Whitby's. One of the Whitby Trustees, Mr Johnson, went post-haste to London to represent to the Commissioners the Trustees' 'most strenuous objections to any union' and to voice the opinion that the contemplated addition of day-places was nonsense, since 'the supply of places in Chichester in the Public Elementary Schools exceeded the demand'. It was apparent to all but the Dean and Chapter on the one hand and Whitby's Trustees on the other that the resources of both schools were being exploited neither to the full nor imaginatively. So, if the Commissioners' plans appear sensible and imaginative, they were naive in supposing that they could readily change the Whitby Trustees from their attitude of self-satisfaction and insularity to one of reconciliation with the Dean and Chapter, who were regarded by the Trustees as the next great enemy after the Commissioners themselves—and the local Dissenters. Nevertheless, the Commissioners persisted, and after months of tedious correspondence and endless delays by the Trustees a meeting was finally fixed for October 1884 at Oliver Whitby's.

As far as the Commissioners were concerned, the meeting with the Trustees was to explain their plans to extend the benefits of the Charity for more imaginative and broader educational purposes. The Trustees, for their part, regarded the visit from a more material angle. The school premises were now old and decrepit, insanitary and overcrowded, and even they felt that the poor could not be expected to be grateful for such inferior accommodation. The Trustees intended, therefore, to persuade the Commissioners of the need to divert some of their invested capital to the rehousing of the school. Mr Ballard prepared a comprehensive and descriptive report of the school as seen through his and the Trustees' eyes. From this, together with evidence given by the Assistant Master and the boys who were at the school, the Commissioners made their report, and it is from their report that we are able to draw a full picture of the daily life and the work of the school at this time.

The school day began at 7 a.m. in the summer and 7.30 a.m. in the winter with the ringing of a hand bell. One or two boys were, by rota, awakened earlier than this in order to clean the schoolroom and the rooms of the Assistant Master. Beds were made by the boys and washing followed, stripped to the waist and in cold water, winter and summer. Next were morning prayers for which the boys knelt on the forms in the dining room. Usually these prayers would consist of extracts of scripture read by the Head Boy 'from a calendar-like book that hung on the back of the main door'. Then came a scripture lesson until breakfast at 8 a.m. Lessons followed at 9.30 a.m. until dinner at 12.30 p.m. Depending on the day and the season, the afternoons were occupied with more lessons, games of cricket or football or a country walk. For their walk the boys marched at a brisk pace, two by two, through the town and were only allowed to walk 'loose' and talk when the City boundary had been reached. After tea at 5.30 p.m. more lessons followed, including learning the catechism or singing, until bedtime at 9 p.m.

For classes the boys were divided into two Divisions and Mr Ballard recorded the syllabus as follows:

<u>Scripture</u>	Div. I and II. Gospel History (with special studies each term, e.g. St Luke). Div. I.O.T. History (study Joshua to end of Solomon's reign). Div. II.O.T. History (from Creation to Joshua).
<u>Reading</u>	Div. I. From the day's Times. Div. II. From an [unknown] Reading Book.
<u>Arithmetic</u>	Div. I. Vulgar and Decimal Fractions: Practice (Simple and Compound) Proportion and its application e.g. Interest, Profit and Loss, Stocks, Discount, Partnership, Equation of Payments etc. Div. II. Simple and Compound Rules, Reduction, Rule of Three and easy Practice.
<u>Mensuration</u>	Div. I. Ordinary surfaces and solids, e.g. Triangles, quadrilaterals, circles, globes, cylinders, parallelepipeds etc. Div. II. None.
<u>Algebra</u>	Div. I. Four Rules and Equations including problems involving fractions with numerical denominator. Div. II. None.
<u>Dictation</u>	Div. I. From the Times. Div. II. An easier piece.
<u>Grammar</u>	Div. I. Parsing, Rules of Syntax and Analysis. Div. II. Easy Parsing.
<u>Literature</u>	Div. I. Special Term by Term, e.g. Trial of Antonio from 'Merchant of Venice'. (This was one of the studies which had to be word perfect to qualify a visit to the annual Sloe Fair held on October 20th.) Div. III. None.
<u>History</u>	Div. I General outlines with dates. Special study for Term e.g. 'Hanoverian Period'. Div. II. None.
<u>Geography</u>	Div. I. General. Special study for Term, e.g. Europe. Div. II. England and Wales and definitions.
<u>Writing</u>	Generally, and specially from Cyphering Books.
<u>Music</u>	Sacred and Secular.
<u>Drawing</u>	Freehand and Practical Geometry.
<u>Drill</u>	Ordinary Military Movements.

The boys' memories of their studies are varied. Handwriting was 'god'. Singing, inspired at one time by a Welsh Assistant Singing Master, was in three parts from tonic sol-fa and, for good measure, a whistlepipe band was started. Most of the Old Boys recalled an obvious emphasis on 'the three R's' and none makes references to any other academic study.

Under a headmaster as irascible as Ballard was, it is to be expected that discipline was severe. The boys were clearly terrified by the man whose temper was at its worst when his beard had been trimmed and 'what little hair he had, cut'. His three favourite maxims, regularly voiced, were 'Train up the child in the way he should go', 'Anything worth doing is worth doing well' and 'Spare the rod and spoil the child'. Three books were kept by the Head Boy, a Black Book for breaches of discipline, a Line Book for faults in clothing and a Lesson Book for errors in lessons. 'Errors' in lessons were entirely due, according to Ballard, to the 'ignorance' or laziness of the boys, and offenders were treated in public to a 'deadly and ironic diatribe' against 'those lazy and indolent ignoramuses whom it is my misfortune to teach'. Caning was for 'trivial offences' and for the more serious offences such as lying or smoking the culprit was made to bend down and be flogged while Ballard gripped the boy's head between his legs. The boys worked hard during any 'spare time' that might occur—they scrubbed the floors, swept, beat mats, attended to the fires and sifted the ashes—and it also appears they were sent on endless errands by Ballard!

Meals were eaten in complete silence surveyed by the headmaster who stood defaulters 'on the mat' and tried to catch those who sought to communicate with each other by using sign language. Neither place nor occasion deterred Ballard from his ruthless reaction if something did not please him. For example, at Morning Service in the Cathedral one of the Cowley Fathers was preaching on the subject of the Immaculate Conception, Ballard rose to his feet and, having said loudly, 'I detest the teachings of this abominable man', gave a signal to the boys to rise and they marched 'clacketty clack' down the aisle and out of the west door. (This colourful description of the boys marching arose from their wearing of hob-nailed boots, a practice of Victorian times to slow down the wearing out of leather soles, which continued at the school, even with shoes, until it closed.)

The Commissioners inquiry into the boys' diet prompted the Trustees to state that they 'had endeavoured to assimilate [it] as far as possible to that of Christ's Hospital' having obtained detail from the school. The Commissioner commented that he was doubtful that the Whitby diet had changed for many years. With the following diet sheet Ballard noted that 'the quantity in each case is practically unlimited'.

Breakfast		Bread and Butter and milk and water.
Tea		Bread and Butter and tea.
Dinner	Sunday	Boiled plum pudding: Leg of Pork, Spare rib, Brisket of Beef or Shoulder of Veal, potatoes and bread.
Monday:		Suet Pudding and treacle: Fresh beef, pork, cold breast of mutton, potatoes and bread.
Tuesday:		Rice: Hash, Salt pork or bacon, occasionally pies, potatoes and bread.
Wednesday:		Suet Puddings and butter: Salt beef, fresh beef or shoulder of veal, potatoes with cabbage, carrots or turnips and bread.
Thursday:		Baked plum puddings made chiefly of the week's pieces of bread: Meat remaining from Wednesday with bacon or pork, potatoes and bread.

Friday: Suet Pudding and treacle: remains of bacon and other meats with tinned canned beef, 'pigs fry', or occasionally pies, potatoes and bread.

Saturday: Homing: Hash, Remains of cold meat, Hot breasts of mutton, potatoes and bread.

To this list Ballard added a comment that a quarter pint of ale was provided in autumn and winter if thought advisable. Also, meals followed the plan of eating pudding first which 'considerably lessens the desire for meat'. Whether this diet sheet was submitted just for the benefit of the Commissioners we cannot know, but Old Boys' memories of the meals and their attitudes to them reflect a different story. All agreed that there was not the variety that Ballard alleged and that there was no change from week to week in the food, apart from the 'occasional' meat pie once a term. Of course, as we would expect, the boys had their pet likes and dislikes and also their own slang for the food. The addition of water to the milk changed it to 'pigeon's milk' and the slabs, as opposed to loaves, of bread were called 'tokes'; the boys would cut off pieces with their personal pocket knives. Since 'waste not want not' was the rule of the school, any boy who failed to clear his plate would be punished. Leaving any of the first course, pudding, would mean no meat to follow. Many boys tell of being unable to cope with the excessive fat on the brisket of beef, known as 'fat junk', and smuggling it out of the dining hall in the ample pockets of their gowns. If caught, the culprit was made to stand in front of the other boys for three meals with plate in hand, fat on plate, and deprived of any food himself. Such luxuries as jam or eggs never appeared. Boys recalled that in blackberry time they would pick berries on afternoon walks, squash them in jam jars and add sugar brought in by one of the boys when he went home with his week's laundry.

There was little to break the monotonous routine of lessons and dull meals except that, very occasionally, some boys were permitted to attend a lecture or concert at the Assembly Room. There was also an annual trip to Brighton, the Crystal Palace or the zoo.

Despite its age and residential nature, the school was at this time without tradition or custom in the conventional sense. For example, none of the Old Boys recalls special treatment of new boys or leavers, they knew little or nothing of their Founder, and even less of the current Trustees. Only two customs appear to have existed—one was to tell new boys that the carved Blue Boy was really one of the boys turned into wood in order to escape punishment when he said, 'God strike me dead if I'm telling a lie'; the other was that every boy should carve his initials somewhere in the school before leaving, a risky practice with a man of Ballard's temper.

Such, then, was the school when Greenwood, an Assistant Charity Commissioner, managed to gain entrance in October 1884. Greenwood records other facts about the school relevant to the main purpose of his visit, which was to examine the state of endowment and to make suitable suggestions for the reallocation of money and the future position of the school. 'He spent considerable time in examining the financial state of the Charity and soon discovered that the Trustees appeared to be singularly lacking in knowledge of the terms of the Charity which they administered, and none seemed to realise that the order passed down to them by The Master of the Rolls in 1826 was in fact an instrument of government. This was particularly so in the matter of paying for apprenticeships; the Trustees were allowed to spend £100, but this was not being carried out. Likewise, 'the trustees were singularly deficient in information' in regard to the property at West Wittering. For example, Whitby had directed in his will that a specific sum of money be set aside for the renewing of the leases of the prebend of West Wittering. This, generations of Trustees had neglected to do and the present Trustees had invested their profits in stock, as provided by the 1826 scheme. They proposed to the Assistant Commissioner that leases of the prebend should be allowed to lapse. This contemplated loss of revenue from tithes was a matter of concern to the Commissioner and his concern, which he registers, seems to mark the turning point in the financial stability of the school.

Greenwood notes the Headmaster's comparatively princely salary of £200 per annum plus house and board, while also observing his competence and efficiency. According to records of the time, the average salary of headmasters was £290 in board schools and £154 in voluntary schools. Taking into account free board and lodgings, Ballard's salary was very good.

Another matter the Assistant Commissioner was not happy with was the proportional representation of the boys. Originally the boys came in equal numbers, four each from Harting, West Wittering and Chichester. But now, with the populations of these three places at 1,274, 655 and 9,652 respectively, the proportions were nine each from Harting and West Wittering and 34 from Chichester. The Trustees tried to explain away this disproportion as a result of the 'low intellectual level' of boys from West Wittering and the great many nonconformists in the parish of Harting. The unequal distribution of the benefit would continue to be a bone of contention for some time.

That Oliver Whitby's School occupied a prestigious position in the eyes of the City cannot be doubted. Places in the school were fiercely competed for, and it is clear from the report that many devices were employed to gain admittance. Parents sought to conceal the fact that they were, for example, members of the 'Wesleyan body' and were therefore ineligible. Clergymen provided certificates for members of their flock testifying their adherence to the Church of England, and then withdrew them upon finding that this claim was 'an apellation of convenience'. Parents moved from outlying villages to reside for 12 months within the City boundary and so qualify for candidature for their children. There is evidence of parents' employers furnishing certificates of weekly earnings, 21s. being looked upon as a maximum. By today's standards this may seem minute and must be set against contemporary prices. Advertisements in the *Chichester Mercury* help here: best rump steak 7d. per pound, 'top of the leg' as used for Ballard's 'occasional pies' 2½d. per pound and cheese 5d. per pound.

On acceptance as candidates, boys were examined and marked 'by impression' on a five-point scale; 'Very good indeed 5: Good 4: Very Fair 3: Fair 2: Moderate 1: Bad 0'. Ballard informed Greenwood, the Assistant Commissioner, that 'the parents of bad boys generally abstain from applying, it being known that a boy not recommended by his school master will be rejected by the Trustees'. Greenwood continued: 'It will be seen from the above that, as the Head Master put it, the Oliver Whitby School provides places in the nature of Scholarships for the Public Elementary Schools, restricted, however, to members of the Church of England.' That Ballard accepted in 1884 the idea of 'higher' learning or better opportunity at his school is noteworthy in the light of his campaign some fifteen years later.

Greenwood had the temerity to question the wisdom of continuing to wear blue gowns (a best gown for Sunday, a second best for walking out and a third for school) and was promptly informed that 'the Trustees are averse to any change in the dress'. They argued that the dress was 'a distinctive feature by which a 'Blue Coat Boy' is at once known in the town and that this tends to prevent breaches of discipline when the boys are away from the school.' This touch of sentiment and emotional unrealism was to prove fatal for the school in its later years and it is amusing to note, at this juncture, that even if the 'town' did have a high opinion of the school and (by inference) its Trustees, they, for their part, were especially critical if not contemptuous of the 'town' and especially the Mayor and City Council.

The Assistant Commissioner noted the absence of science from the curriculum and also made reference to the *ab initio* provisions for the teaching of navigation. He was informed that 'few if any of the boys go to sea. They are too highly educated and prefer employment in offices, business establishments and the like.' That a white-collar job was regarded as the height of ambition was echoed in the opinion of the Headmaster who said that 'there was insufficient time for technical instruction' and that 'a general education was preferred as being the most suitable for employment and clerkship'.

The buildings were, in Greenwood's view, badly overcrowded and the dormitories, whilst 'being 'neat and clean and airy', were draughty and cold.

Most of Greenwood's views were accepted by the Trustees with a show of 'passive resistance' for they clung firmly to their belief that their ideas and management, put into practical form by Ballard, were beyond criticism. When, however, the question of the constitution of the school was raised, the Trustees became 'active' in the extreme. With incredible perversity they regarded suggestions for changes as personal attacks upon themselves. It was suggested that day-boys be admitted, but this was countered by the view that such boys would not be under full control of the Master and would thus 'demoralise' the boarders. When the question of 'intermediate education' was raised, the Trustees argued, with sublime illogicality, that their own school was 'considerably above the Elementary grade' and that 'the people of Chichester would object to any change and would no longer have such faith as at present in. the boys educated at the School'. The biggest bone of contention was the question of additional Trustees or Governors, especially if a member of the Dean and Chapter was proposed. The Trustees, reported Greenwood, say 'that they take great interest in the foundation and work together harmoniously, and whether or not their resignation would be to the advantage of the school or the county, to resign they would be compelled if they were to be associated with a representative element.' The final straw was that nonconformist boarders should be admitted if their parents agreed to their receiving Church of England doctrinal teaching. In despair Greenwood summed up:

> The Trustees, however, would object to this as to all other suggested change, and it appears to me in the face of their objections, and in view of the strict terms of the instrument of foundations, it will be difficult to introduce extensive alterations in the administration of the Charity. I cannot doubt that the school is well and conscientiously managed and is doing good work within the narrow limits assigned to it. How far these limits can be extended and how far it would be expedient to extend them must be a subject for much consideration. Possibly it would be advisable to ascertain what is the prevalent opinion among those best to judge in the town upon that subject.

For the first time in a new and expanding age of education, opportunity presented itself to the Oliver Whitby School Trustees, but they neither heeded the advice nor compared themselves with other schools such as Christ's Hospital, Westminster Grey Coat, and the Norwich Girls' Hospital schools, whose historical similarity was at least relevant to their own situation. Greenwood had hoped for an opinion from those locally 'qualified to judge'. In the following years two such appeared, one a man of substance, the other a man of straw, but, as we shall see, neither 'qualified' in the eyes of the Trustees to take cognisance of their 'precious' school.

The Charity Commissioners achieved nothing except to persuade, unbelievable as it may seem, the Trustees to transfer the funds to the Commissioners who would pay dividends to the Trustees' accounts. If Chichester's drains were to be the 'grave' for the Oliver Whitby School, then the Minute by which the funds were transferred was the first 'nail in the coffin'.

It was at this time, 1884, that an incident of truly Dickensian proportions, even to the name of the main protagonist, occurred. Although not directly affecting the history of the school, it nevertheless served to increase the Trustees' sense of self-righteousness and to harden their already impervious minds. Charles Snuggs was Vestry Clerk of the parish of West Wittering and saw himself as a guardian of the rights and privileges of the parish. In the beginning Chichester, Harting and West Wittering sent equal numbers of boys to Oliver Whitby's School. However, in 1884 and subsequently, this was no longer so. Moreover, the entire revenue of the school derived from land and property in West Wittering, but no resident of West Wittering had ever been a Trustee. In the eyes of Charles Snuggs it followed that the Trustees of the school were 'wicked men'—they exploited the benefits of the charity to their own and everybody else's good to the disregard and detriment of the good people of Wittering.

When Snuggs failed to get any private satisfaction from the Trustees, he sought to do battle publicly and, in November 1886, addressed a militant letter to *The Daily News*, complaining of the unfairness of the Trustees in providing only eight places for West Wittering boys in the school out of a total of fifty-two. A copy of this letter reached the office of the Charity Commissioners and coincided with a visit there of Mr Ballard on an entirely different matter. As one may expect, Ballard was frustrated by Snuggs' allegations and told the Commissioners that Snuggs was 'a cantankerous old man who carried no weight at all and was all wrong'. The Commissioners, no doubt, had more to occupy their minds than dealing with the biased opinions of a Vestry Clerk. But in Snuggs they met a tireless campaigner. For two years he plied London with correspondence and, although the Commissioners had, in 1884, satisfied themselves as to the administrative integrity of the school but had failed to carry a case for expansion, with Snuggs' persistence as an 'excuse' they found the means of making contact with the 'enemy' once more. They managed to gain for themselves further information about the school, culminating in 1891 with another meeting with the Trustees. With Snuggs as the immediate reason for their enquiry, they acquired from the Trustees information which in part they related to the Vestry Clerk to fuel his feud whilst, at the same time, arming themselves with material or 'weapons' for their own subsequent 'attack'.

Snuggs complained of the small number of boys participating in the Charity, which was also a complaint of the Commissioners. Snuggs, of course, had in mind a more liberal representation from his own parish, whereas the Commissioners sought a more general spread. He then challenged the 'type' of boys attending the school and their places of residence. This prompted the Commissioners to obtain from the Trustees a full list of boys attending the school with a note of their places of residence and family income, which revealed, in fact, that the Trustees were not as careful as they had alleged to Greenwood in 1884 as some of the boys were not residents in the City. But to Snuggs the Commissioners wrote that all was managed according to the Chancery Scheme of 1826 and that they would not contemplate an inquiry since there had been one in 1884. Snuggs, like a terrier, would not let go of his prey. Allegations of favouritism, harshness on the part of the Master, acceptance of wealthy boys, misappropriation of funds continued to pour in until, in desperation, the Charity Commissioners agreed to send to Chichester an assistant, one A.C. Eddis, to hold a public inquiry on 20 July 1891.

Snuggs mustered his forces and brought support, in letter form, from the Bishop of Chichester and by their presence his own vicar and many farmers. One can imagine the inquiry being like a visit to the D'Oyly Carte, as Eddis, after hearing all the complaints and evidence, recorded that there was 'I think, no tangible complaint against the administration of the Charity as far as West Wittering is concerned'. Eddis also wrote:

> I may premise by 'saying that Mr. Snuggs is a man of a very pugnacious disposition. As I gathered at the meeting he is always fighting some person or institution. He is now engaged in opposing some new drainage scheme which, it is anticipated, will procure a respite for the Oliver Whitby's Charity. Mr Snuggs is unfortunately very deaf, and I think it is not at all impossible that he does not accurately hear what is said but puts his own version on it and then is impervious to explanation or argument.

The outcome for the Charity Commissioners was fruitful for, delighted as the Trustees were in their success, they agreed to meet Mr Eddis in the autumn to discuss again the future of the school. Though Snuggs had lost the round, Eddis's fears were fulfilled. Questions in the House were threatened; the Commissioners were accused of shielding the Trustees and finally the Lord Chancellor was addressed. The Commissioners did no more, however, and Snuggs ceased his pestering when Chichester's inevitable drainage problem demanded his attention.

Before considering in detail the next meeting between the Charity Commissioners and Whitby's Trustees, it is only right that we briefly look at the material state of the school on the one hand and, on the other, the changed and changing educational scene at the national level which accounts, in some measure, for the persistent interest of the Commissioners.

Between the years 1884 and 1891 the school continued under Ballard's unswerving guidance. The annual trip was made to the Crystal Palace and several lectures, magic lantern shows and otherwise, were attended. In 1886 a total of £25 6s. 11d., a record expenditure, was made on new books for the school. Also in this year Miss Linton, matron for 17 years, received 'a gift of £50' upon her retirement. According to the Minutes of these years the boys were regularly arraigned before the Trustees for being 'idle and lazy', some on occasions being expelled. However, the most disturbing entries are those which reveal the Trustees' concern at falling income and the subsequent decrease in the numbers of boys attending the school.

In the national arena the need for secondary education was being recognised. Within the field of elementary education considerable progress had been made since 1870. Between then and 1876 accommodation in inspected schools had risen from about two million to three and a half million. This increase in school places, coupled with the fact that some 52 per cent of the population were subject to bye-laws made by local school-boards about compulsory attendance, enabled Disraeli's government, in 1876, to take a step towards universal compulsory attendance. The step was completed by the Act of 1880 whereby the making of bye-laws was compulsory for school-boards and school attendance committees.

Simultaneously men's minds were occupied by the growing 'rivalry' of public (rate-aided) and voluntary schools. The situation is well summed up by Leach: 'Whilst opinion was maturing on this topic [free education], there began to force itself upon the public mind the vastly more difficult problem of combining the two systems of voluntary, denominational, state-aided schools on the one hand, and public, non-denominational rate supported schools on the other.' From the denominational point of view, the problem appeared as a burden imposed and a danger threatened in ever-increasing degree by the competition of the board schools. This competition was felt not so much by direct rivalry of school with school as indirectly by the steady raising of the standard of efficiency with respect to buildings, equipment, salaries of teachers and educational attainment—inevitable results from the establishment of authorities with power to draw upon the rates. On the other hand, from the purely educational point of view, the dual system tended in practice to an illicit but almost inevitable recognition of two standards of efficiency, the lower being conceded to voluntary schools in consideration of their comparative 'poverty'. Some ten years later the Cross Commission surveyed the whole state of elementary education including higher-grade schools and agreed that a more liberal curriculum was necessary. With the Local Government Act of 1888 many of the ideas of the Technical Instruction Acts could be put into practical operation. Finally the Education Act of 1891 abolished the payment of fees for children above the age of three and under fifteen.

In the field of 'secondary' education the Oliver Whitby School's avoidance of early commissions has been noted. Events, however, in the national field were moving fast, though during the years following the passing of the Local Government Act in 1888, by which County Councils were set up, there is little of the magnitude affecting education of the Act of 1870 or, in the future, the Act of 1902. Nevertheless, legislation concerning the 'higher' or post-elementary fields of education all served in Chichester to push the Whitby school into a backwater and to lessen the academic esteem in which it had been held for so many years. Of the legislation, the Technical Instruction Act of 1889 was important. It allowed the Councils to supply, or aid the supply of, technical or manual instruction and to delegate authority for this to a special committee appointed wholly or partly from its members.

By the time, therefore, that Eddis returned to Chichester in October 1891, the tide was beginning to flow against Oliver Whitby's School. In the first place the Trustees had lost their immediate hold over their finances. Secondly, loss of income lowered the number of boys in the school; in fact it never again reached, let alone passed, the total of 52 at the time of Commissioner Greenwood's visit in 1884. Thirdly, discipline and residence apart, it was no longer apparent that the Whitby School was giving 'the best education' in Chichester. Fourthly, there were those in the City who sought to take advantage of powers under the Local Government Act to further 'secondary' education in a rather general sense.

Eddis again met the Trustees of Whitby's School on 21 October 1891. Though, presumably, he had parted from them in the summer on reasonably amicable terms, he knew from the failures of his predecessors—the tone of the correspondence relative to Snugg's complaints, and Ballard's public display of temper at the inquiry at Wittering, when he was declared to be harsh and bullying—that the task before him was not easy. At the same time the general vagueness on the part of the Trustees, which Greenwood had noted, persuaded him to hope that, though resentful of attacks on their personal integrity, their knowledge of education was such that they would be indifferent to educational changes in their school. So with none of the temerity of the angels Eddis suggested to the assembled Trustees, accompanied by their Clerk and Headmaster, that:

1) Day boys should be introduced.
2) Technical education should be developed.
3) Alterations should be made in the nature of the government of the school to admit representation of such bodies as the Dean and Chapter, and the City and County Councils.

It was a considerably chastened Commissioner who recorded in his report: 'I had expected to meet with considerable indifference ... but instead I had to encounter the most strenuous opposition of the whole body to any alteration.' Eddis had gone there in honesty 'to ascertain, whether any steps could be taken to improve the application of the funds of the Foundation so as to render it more conducive to the advancement of education in Chichester, even to the extent of altering, consistent with the main designs of the Founder, the lines on which it [was] being administered.' Some twenty years before, the Schools Inquiry Commission in prophetic mantle had realised that the possession of an endowment in a rural locality could operate not infrequently to prevent the establishment of an efficient state-aided school. Nowhere was this more true than in Chichester where Oliver Whitby's Trustees, patently ignorant of many of the clauses of their Founder's will, were equally adamant as to the rightness of their interpretation of their Founder's spirit and intention in a changing educational scene within a contemporary society.

The Trustees, in their resentment of 'interference', based all their objections on an initial false premise or misunderstanding. They were incapable of comprehending the simple fact that the school *per se* was not under attack. The fact was that its standards were appraised and admired. No one questioned that 'they were doing a good job' or doubted that the impressive list of lucrative posts to which 'Old Boys' succeeded was not sufficient evidence of the high spiritual values and academic integrity of the pupils. But the fact remained that the school was a 'closed shop'. Outside 'interference' merely aimed at a means of making a good school better, together with a wider spread of the Foundation's favours, but this the Trustees could not or would not see.

To the suggested introduction of day-boys the Trustees countered as follows: in the first place more staff would be needed and this they could not afford. Secondly, they admitted that as 'almost as good an education was now provided in the Public Elementary School', parents would be reluctant to pay and they (the Trustees), for their part, 'could not bear so great a strain on the already decreased income of the Charity'. Moreover, in their view the boarding element was supremely beneficial. If day-boys were admitted they would return 'to their squalid surroundings' and discipline would be impossible with 'freedom for one part of the school and restraint for the boarders'.

Eddis countered that fee-paying at an economic figure was clearly the answer, but this the Trustees declined to consider since 'the higher social standing of possible fee payers would cause them to look down on the boarders and there would be introduced an element of discontent and social antagonism'. For men whose social antagonisms were rabid such a statement smacks of hypocrisy.

It was clear to Eddis that the Trustees never once considered that they might 'supply' education in advance of 'demand', as indeed Oliver Whitby himself had provided. There was, asserted the Trustees, 'no demand for Technical Education in Chichester' nor was there 'a demand for intermediate education in Chichester'. It is difficult to know the Trustees' authority for these statements. More likely their rider that 'in respect of Technical Education they would not under any circumstances apply to the County or Town Councils' conceals their true feelings: that they would not have any dealings with trumped up butchers, bakers and candlestick makers who presumed to 'govern' locally those who were their social superiors.

As one may deduce, tempers ran high on these issues, but it was nothing to the explosion point reached on the matter of changes in the government of the school. 'This suggestion', wrote the despairing Eddis, 'the Trustees oppose more vehemently than others'. Their position as Trustees was frequently 'handed on from father to son', they 'had no financial gain' so that, concluded Eddis, 'their objections to all change rendered a consideration of details superfluous'. The final broadside was fired by Mr Smith, a Senior Trustee. 'While they recognised', he said, 'the force of law and would bow to it, and while they did not question the right of the Charity Commission to make a scheme affecting the school, they declined to render any assistance, and, in the event of the Charity Commission deciding to take any steps in that direction, their intention was to retire.' So the meeting closed. Nothing was accomplished, another nail was driven into the coffin of Oliver Whitby's School, and a further barrier erected in Chichester on the road towards secondary education.

On his previous visit to Chichester Eddis had been sympathetically impressed by Ballard. He therefore sought from the Headmaster his personal views on the matter. From Ballard the, by now, despairing and disconsolate Commissioner gained no encouragement. Ballard confirmed that 'there is little or no desire for intermediate education in Chichester' and that 'the Public Elementary schools would resent the withdrawal of their best scholars as this would prejudice their grant.'

1891 came to a close and the boys were examined at Christmas by a new examiner, Mr J. Parsons. They went home for the Christmas holidays, almost certainly oblivious that discussions about the school and its future had taken place. Setting aside Snuggs' eccentric interest, few if any of Chichester's residents had the slightest interest in the school beyond an emotional attachment to its presence within the City. Although the school drew the majority of its boys from the City, it could hardly be regarded as an integral part of City life. This cloistered existence stemmed, no doubt, from Mr Ballard's unrelenting discipline and his resolve that his boys should in no way be 'contaminated' by contact with a wicked outside world. Moreover, the Trustees themselves were 'men apart' from the life of the City and, assured of the competence and wisdom of their administration and bolstered by what they considered to be a sufficiency of capital, they could imagine no reason for changing their school.

Of course, the good people of Chichester were aware of the 'Blue Coat Boys'. They attended Divine Service every Sunday in the Cathedral, even if Oxford Movement tendencies were an irritation to their Headmaster. They were also to be seen marching briskly through the City to their Sunday afternoon walk or taking part in the annual revels of the Ancient Order of Foresters. But, these activities apart, the affairs of the Oliver Whitby School were not 'news'. During Mr Pescod's time there were frequent mentions of the boys in local papers, but with Mr Ballard at the helm neither the *West Sussex Gazette*, *Chichester Observer* nor *Hampshire Telegraph* notices the boys' existence although activities of The Prebendal School, Lancastrian School and other 'private' schools receive full and frequent mentions.

Education in general was, however, regular news in the local papers. Apart from local activities and disputes about the Godlessness of Board Schools, such items as—the working of School Attendance Committees, the relative quality of Voluntary Schools *vis-à-vis* Board Schools, the provision of the Technical Instruction Acts and use of Science and Art Department Grants—all received more than ample coverage and editorial comment. A reader would scarcely register the fact that there was the Whitby School in Chichester. This extreme isolation and the suppression of possible means of extending benefits had concerned central authority since the Schools Inquiry Commission and is a constantly recurring theme of both Greenwood's and Eddis's reports.

The day of reckoning was drawing near, though at the time the Trustees saw it only as the final victory against their would-be local and national reformers. The final destiny of the Oliver Whitby School was determined in 1897. However, before we discuss in detail the events of that year, we must set the local scene and, very briefly, the national educational picture.

Visually Chichester had changed little. The streets were still unpaved, though markets were no longer held in them. Gas lighting shed some feeble illumination at the street corners. Somertown and St Pancras teemed with low life and were barely safe to walk through alone. Here the locals did battle with the Salvation Army's 'Flying Squadron', meeting 'the word of the spirit' with cabbages, eggs and rotten marrow. In the City itself there was a total of 102 public houses, representing one per 79 members (adult and juvenile) of the population. This proportion was only surpassed by seven other cities, towns or boroughs in the whole of the Kingdom. The City Cross was decaying and needed repair, the City Walls seemed an encumbrance and a movement was afoot to destroy them. The Cathedral repented of its earlier reforming zeal in destroying the great choir screen, and placed at the junction of nave and choir a wooden memorial to 'a beloved Archdeacon'. Speculative building was slowly joining the south-east part of the City to the ancient hamlet of Wyke. Gracious Georgian buildings still faced the main streets and filled many of the side streets. The Militia came and went, poachers were charged, drunks were apprehended, deserters caught hiding between a brace of feather beds in the *Coach and Horses* and the aged Bishop Durnford still ruled the See and thundered occasionally against High Church extremes of the Brighton clergy.

In the decade before 1897, whilst Chichester's *status quo* in all aspects of life remained, two men and one cause dominate the scene. Neither of the men was directly concerned with Oliver Whitby's School nor was the cause they contended connected with it. Yet it is from their struggle that the subsequent history of the school derives.

Ebenezer Prior lived in what is now Tower Street, not so many doors away from the school and Mr Ballard. A wool merchant, as his forbears had been, he was comparatively wealthy and generous in support of social causes. A Congregationalist, a teetotaller and a member of the City Guardians, he achieved considerable unpopularity in 1889 by challenging the quantity of drink served in the workhouse. As a result of a Public Inquiry, Pullinger, the Relieving Officer, was suspended. The public houses were a constant object of his attack. In his opinion they were 'low in tone', frequently 'houses of ill repute' and 'dens of gambling and drunkenness'. He did all in his power to suspend licences and reduce the number of inns in the City. However, it was the unhygienic state of Chichester which agitated him beyond measure. The street pumps provided water that was 'coffee coloured' or 'stank' and 'cesspits overflowed into cellars'.

Arthur Bostock, M.R.C.S., lived in St John's Street in a house with a basement and three floors, well ministered to by generations of grateful and deferential servants. When the gentry were ill, he it was whom they called, only deigning to bring in Dr Buckell or his modern-minded doctor-sons when Bostock wanted 'a second opinion'. Nominally a member of the Church of England, Bostock was, above all, Mayor of Chichester for many years. On medical grounds he saw no reason to agitate for an improvement in the City's sanitary state and, for personal motives quite beyond comprehension, saw no reason to jeopardise his position of petty power by campaigning for schemes that could only bring a 'crippling' increase in the rates.

However, on the matter of Chichester's drains, Prior determined to do battle and so made, in Bostock, a life-long and bitter enemy. For some 25 years the generally insanitary state of the City had been of concern and the record of epidemics was consistent. So it was during 1889 that Prior, who was not then a member of the City Council, opened his attack. Bostock countered with an issue of handbills throughout the City, and on 25 September 1889 held the first of a great series of public meetings against the drains and the 'drainers', as Prior's party which included Dr Buckell came to be known. In November came the annual election for City councillors and there was but one issue on which to fight the election—the drains!

Hygiene and health are not things to be 'seen' in the broadest sense. Pennies on the rates are. So on financial grounds, spurious medical grounds, arguments that 'cheaper ways can be found of dealing with the problem' and 'property will definitely decrease in value if main drained', Bostock, relying on his personal popularity as the kindly, riding-to-hounds, enjoying good-living, medical mayor, won the election and severely trounced Prior 'the puritan preacher' and his party. 'So', impatiently the editor of the *Observer* wrote, 'a majority of the inhabitants decided that the time for uniting cleanliness with Godliness in a cathedral city had not yet arrived.' As on previous occasions some of Chichester's domestic difficulties had attained national prominence, so now both the *Lancet* and The British Medical Association were trenchant in their criticism of 'local medical opinion'.

Though Prior was defeated that November, fate conspired to enable him to gain a place on the City Council through a by-election. Now the attacks could take place within the enemy's ranks, which they did for three long years, with Prior campaigning almost daily for the drainage of the City. Schemes and counter-schemes were put forward until, at a public meeting of the Sanitary Association, it was resolved to petition 'the Local Government Board in London' about the Council's negligence. A public enquiry was ordered and held, the results being published on 15 June 1892. London decided that main drainage must be carried out or else a compulsory order would be applied. Still nothing happened and Prior publicly condemned Dr Bostock by name at a meeting of The Sanitary Association on 28 September. But Chichester was committed and with the aid of a loan the old evils of cesspits and soak-away drains were finally removed. As a result of all this, the animosity of Bostock towards Prior and Chichester's financial embarrassment were to prove mortal as far as Oliver Whitby's School was concerned.

If progress in general moved forward slowly in Chichester and in educational terms appeared to move forward not at all, at the national level progress, if not quick, was at least constant. In October 1892 the Vice Chancellor of Oxford convened a conference on secondary education in England and, partly as a result of this conference, in 1894 the Government appointed a Royal Commission on the subject. This Commission, under the chairmanship of Mr Bryce, had as its terms of reference 'to consider what are the best methods of establishing a well organised system of secondary education in England, taking into account existing deficiencies, and having regard to such local sources of revenue from endowments or otherwise as are available or may be made available for this purpose and to make recommendations accordingly.'

The Spens Report was published in 1895 and many of the general recommendations are of extreme importance when applied to the educational scene in Chichester at the time. 'In regard to the provision of secondary schools, the first principle should be to utilise every existing element of the supply which was, or could be made, good of its kind. It was desirable, for instance, to utilise all those private schools which were really efficient and which accepted public tests of efficiency.' Material matters such as 'supply and demand' of secondary places apart, the Commission had much to say on the 'spiritual' matter of true education. It stressed again and again the fact that, 'The largest of the problems which concern the future of secondary education is how to secure, as far as possible, that in all schools and every branch of study the pupils shall not only be instructed but educated'.

It so happens that, before the publication of the Royal Commissioner's Report, Chichester's advocate for reform, Ebenezer Prior, had been turning his attention to the lack of secondary education in the City. On 8 June 1894 The City Council resolved to appoint a Charities Committee to enquire into the use and administration of Chichester's three principal charities, The Oliver Whitby School, The Prebendal School and St Mary's Hospital. In October of that year they applied themselves fully to their task and addressed the authorities concerned but with no success. During the winter and early spring of the following year Prior pestered the Whitby Trustees and the Dean and Chapter, until on 6 May he persuaded the City's Technical Instruction Committee to resolve to apply to the Charity Commissioners requesting them to hold a general inquiry 'into all the existing charities in Chichester with a view to their being utilised for the public benefit to a greater extent than at present'. This resolution of the Committee, chaired by Prior who was now Mayor of Chichester, was confirmed by the full Council on 17 May and a letter requesting such an inquiry was sent to the Charity Commissioner from whom came a disappointing reply: 'The Commissioners would hesitate to undertake an inquiry of such magnitude unless upon some definite suggestion of maladministration or neglect.' As such an allegation could not be made, for the time being at least, this line of attack seemed closed.

By now old Bishop Durnford was dead, and when the Finance Committee of the City Council met on 19 January 1896 their main concern was to approve an address to his successor on the occasion of his enthronement. This address contained the following passage: 'Especially we desire to call your Lordship's attention to the Charities and the Scholastic Institutions in the City; the Charities may with wiser administration be of much greater advantage to the poor, and the schools may be improved and extended so that the Citizens in their several degrees may be more fully qualified to meet the requirements of the present day.' Ardent as was Prior's desire for reform, he nonetheless felt that blatant reference, on an occasion when many members of the charities under attack were sitting at Lunch as guests of the City, would be in extreme bad taste and so he persuaded the Committee to expunge all direct reference to particular Charities.

It was agreed, however, that Prior, as Mayor, should meet the new Bishop and 'acquaint the Bishop as to the Council's views'. They met, with Prior stressing the earnest desire of the City Council to work with the Church and he outlined his plans for the Oliver Whitby School. During the months of March and April 1896 the local press, in particular the *Chichester Observer*, *West Sussex Gazette* and the *Sussex Daily News*, all voiced complaints as to the inadequacy of 'technical instruction' in Chichester. Through the influence of Dufton, Inspector of the Science and Art Department for the South East District, Prior obtained an interview with one of the Charity Commissioners, a Mr Richmond, and outlined his scheme. Richmond was more than sympathetic and said that 'the Commissioners had consistently endeavoured as far as they could to change these closed hospital schools into large day schools and instanced Westminster School, but that having regard to the admittedly excellent management of the school etc. an approach to the Trustees was suggested.' He warned Prior, moreover, that he would be attacked for 'robbing the poor' and pointed out to him the need to protect the outlying parishes from any invasion of their rights. It must have been with a heavy heart that Prior left Richmond. Where Greenwood and Eddis had failed, what could he hope to achieve? This, Richmond must have known as well, but he lacked the powers of compulsion to alter a state of affairs where earlier persuasion had achieved nothing.

Prior returned and campaigned for his scheme that the Oliver Whitby School should provide free education for its 48 'foundation scholars' with money in lieu of board, and places for upwards of two hundred fee-paying scholars. Despite all that had been said, Prior was unable to meet Smith, Chairman of the Whitby Trustees, until 2 January 1897. He met the same sort of rebuff as Eddis had received some years earlier and was told that the Trustees would not agree to a change of management of the Charity, 'but if the Commissioners insisted, then the Trustees would not desire to be part of the new Governing body'.

By now Prior had worked out his scheme to the full. On 10 February he placed it before the City 'Technical Committee' who approved it with the proviso that it should be discussed with County Authorities. In March the Chairman of the County Technical Committee wrote to the Charity Commissioners to say he had met Prior and was 'favourable' to the proposal. So the scheme was printed and distributed and, after copies had been sent to London, it appeared in local papers on 18 and 25 February. Prior also had a letter published in the local press: 'I anticipate nothing can add more to the lustre of our ancient city, than to make her the centre of an educational area ... Surely it is an ambition worthy of any Cicestrian to quicken the vitality of an old school and to enormously extend its usefulness in days when the work it can do is beyond measure important.'

Prior aimed at widening the scope of the school by the addition of paying scholars, and also sought to replace the five Trustees by a governing body of 12 of whom two should be nominated by the County Council and four by the City. As for the religious bar which was operated in respect of the Trustees by the will of the founder, Prior now believed that it should be waived by the new governing body. He wished the foundation to include an expanded boys' school of no fewer than one hundred and fifty scholars and a new girls' school of no fewer than one hundred and twenty-five. The Master should be a member of the Church of England and preferably a graduate, but it was not necessary for him to be in Holy Orders. The scholars should be at least nine and not more than sixteen and fees not less than £6 nor more than £12 per annum. All religious instruction should be according to the doctrines of the Church of England but a 'conscience clause' should be included. The

48 boys of the Foundation should have free places and receive £9 per annum in lieu of board. The election of Foundation scholars was the prerogative of the governors. Finally, if the present Headmaster was not elected as Head of the new school he was 'to get liberal compensation in consequence of his great services'.

Chichester was flabbergasted that anyone should dare to tamper with the Oliver Whitby School, least of all Mr Prior, who was notorious for his strict manner of life and still unpopular because of his campaigns against abuse at the workhouse and for main drainage.

However, Prior too had his supporters and none was more loyal or prejudiced in his favour than the *West Sussex Gazette*. When counter-attacks began on 25 February, the *Gazette's* leader commented: 'The public need council and guidance—not sentiment, and particularly sentiment of the sort stirred up by Mr. Bew in another column.' Mr Bew was the great hope of the anti-Prior faction: a solicitor, and most important of all he was an Old Oliver Whitbyian. He could not and would not see that the subject of debate was simply its possible future and not the school's past and present. He opened his attacks on Prior by shouting 'hands off the birthright of the poor' and 'beware attacks on the Church of England'. Mr Bew continued: 'I honestly respect all nonconformists; but I think even Mr. Prior would groan if the endow-ment of his chapel were purposed to be used for the benefit of say, *inter alia*, Roman Catholics. For really no reason at all is this to be done. I beg pardon. Mr Prior thinks it should be. What greater reason could one wish?' The battle raged, and in letters published in March a majority of the City Council joined in the public outcry against Mr Prior.

Still the *Gazette* remained loyal to Prior and carried a leader of merit on 11 March. Those who are against the scheme are rightly attached to the school but,

> because, as they have never known a good public secondary school in their midst, nor lived outside Chichester's needs as manifested to them in their own experience, they are necessarily less able than others to form a valuable opinion on the gain such a school would be to the City. There is something pathetic in letters from 'old boys' who unconsciously and plainly shew that they do not know what secondary education is nor have even set their minds to the solution of the problem. How can we do for Chichester's sons and daughters today that which Oliver Whitby did for the Chichester of his day? Under this scheme is it fair to say that the poor are robbed of their school? The poor today have an educational outfit *free* of which Oliver Whitby never dreamed. An efficient public secondary school in Chichester will do more for that City than any other investment.

Attackers, such as R.F. Collins an Old Boy, cited the way in which middle-class boys were pushing the poor out of Christ's Hospital and still the *Gazette* countered, and pleaded that Oliver Whitby would say, 'Prove that you know me now, by doing today what 1 did in my day. Is this too difficult for his friends?' Mr Shippam (of potted meat fame) was rebuked for suggesting that secondary education was not needed: 'Where do Mr Shippam and his friends similarly circumstanced send their children?' Others, such as Councillor Aylmore, were severely censured by comments to the effect that they 'scarcely grasped one admirable feature of the scheme'. The Dean and Chapter praised the idea of secondary education but 'would resist to the utmost any interference' with the Whitby School. The patient Prior could not refrain from reminding the Canons, in a letter of 15 April 1897, of their flat disinterest in their own Prebendal School.

By this time the Charity Commissioners were fully aware of the developing situation in Chichester, for not only were they in possession of Prior's scheme but also received him on many occasions to give him advice and support. All arguments he countered with calm and reason. His critics urged that the Church would lose control; he pointed out that they never had control, but if his scheme was successful then the Church of England control might be tightened for the clergy might be included on the new governing board. Attacked as he was, Prior never lost sight of his objective and sought every opportunity to remind everyone of his earnest wish: 'I and my friends are solely activated by the earnest desire, I might almost say determination to get Secondary Education for Chichester and its district.' Again, Chichester's battle received national coverage in the press; from as far afield as Perthshire, support arrived from a Rev. W.M. Meredith. By June 1897 Prior felt that the situation was changing in his favour and, acting now as an individual, asked for a Public Inquiry. Eddis was told, in reply to his own memorandum to Sir George Young, 'Mr. Prior is so deserving of our support that I incline to take his advise and send you down to make an informal public inquiry.'

Eddis then wrote to Prior, who booked the Assembly Room for the meeting on 22 July at 6 p.m. Typically, the Trustees of Oliver Whitby's School found this time inconvenient. Bew's wrath now knew no bounds and he wrote complaining to the Charity Commissioners. They replied to him and the Whitby Trustees, pointing out firmly that 'the Inquiry is not into the past administration', but that now, 'It is the desire of the Commissioners that the matter should be further inquired into, but they do not at this stage commit themselves to any proposals on their own account.'

Bew, the 'Old Oliver Whitbyian', was distinctly unhappy according to the *Chichester Observer* which sympathetically suggested that, whereas he might be a good lawyer, he needed a person of substance to lend weight to his campaign and unite his diverse supporters. Who more suitable could he find, and who more willing, than Prior's old personal enemy, the former Mayor and favourite of rich and poor, Bostock? So once more Bostock entered the lists with Prior. Whereas Bew continued to be almost paranoid about the competence of the administration, Bostock, a master of strategy, relied on uniting round himself a body of antagonists who represented all shades of social standing from the Lord Bishop down-wards. Notices appeared throughout Chichester inviting the public to 'Come in numbers to protest' at a meeting to be held on Monday 19th, three days before the official Public Inquiry. Moreover, 'the public [were] invited to sign a memorial to the Charity Commission now lying for signature at the Stationers, Printers and others'. This meeting was a huge success; some six hundred people attended who 'most respectfully protested against any interference with or disturbance of the present funds of the Oliver Whitby School in the said City', and this resolution, with a memorial of one thousand signatures, was received in London on Wednesday 21 July.

Meanwhile, Bew had launched a highly emotional attack on Prior at a meeting of the City Council and carried a resolution that 'This council is entirely opposed to any alteration or interference with the management and funds of Oliver Whitby's school'. 'Who was it', he fulminated,

> that was not content with bossing the Technical Committee, not content with breaking the confidence of Committee work and who was now assuming to boss the Charity Commissioners? Mr. Eb. Prior! Let it be understood that it was Mr. Prior of Tower Street who was doing all this mischief for mischief it really was ... The benefits were to be extended to that class which did not want them ... Someone has gone behind our backs and brought an Assistant Charity Commissioner on the scene ... join with me in the cry 'Hands Off'.

The resolution being put was seconded by Alderman Garland who observed, in the best spirit of Sir Roger de Coverley, that 'it would be dangerous to start tampering with the foundation because they could not forsee where it would end'.

It must have been with considerable trepidation that Eddis set out from London on the morning of Thursday 22 July 1897 for his third visit to Chichester. Well acquainted with the Whitby School and its past history, he had personal experience of the intransigence of the Trustees. He knew Prior as 'a man of great enthusiasm' and he knew of the bitter enmity of Bostock because of the drainage business. Likewise, he knew that Prior was unpopular because of his attacks on the mismanagement of the workhouse. However, armed with the many petitions and memorials, he arrived in Chichester and opened the meeting at 6 p.m. in the Assembly Room.

Imagine the scene set before him: on the one hand Prior and his supporters including Dufton the Science and Art Department Inspector, Young, organising Secretary for Technical Education, and Marshall, the Headmaster of Brighton Grammar School. On the other side Bostock, Bew, the Dean and Chapter, a majority of the City Council, Ballard and the Trustees. The room itself was full of people 'who represented the drinking part of the population and who had gone ... urged to by others ... for the purpose of shouting down Mr. Prior and his supporters'. Eddis opened by explaining the purpose of the meeting and, having pleaded with his audience to 'keep down the temperature and their tempers', called on Prior to speak.

Prior outlined the history of his scheme and cited as an example the treatment of The Peter Symonds' Charity in Winchester (1894) as a successful handling of a 'closed' Church of England charity. So great was the desire of the nonconformists in Chichester for secondary education, he said, that they would not oppose the extension of Church of England teaching to 250 children. He concluded in tones of considerable dignity and statesmanship:

> It is true that the founder [of Oliver Whitby's School] was before his age. It is true that he did not anticipate as many as 48 being on the foundation, but do you think a man so advanced as he was, would rejoice to feel that only 48 boys receiving the full amount of their food and clothing and a much more liberal education, but that through the medium of his benefaction the priceless benefit of a splendid education was extended to 250 boys and girls in this part of West Sussex? I submit that the best possible education is the heritage of Englishmen. I submit that England will not maintain her place against the competition of the world unless she is eager in education as other nations are. I maintain that the children of working men with exceptional ability, the picked ones, that is, should have a complete educational ladder from the elementary school to the University put within their grasp.

For three and a half hours the battle raged. All the old objections were raised, the rights of the poor, denominational 'poaching' of Church money, whilst Prior's supporters were interrupted and shouted down. Eddis, said the *West Sussex Gazette*, 'got nothing he did not know before, save indeed that Chichester contains some who prefer the riots of primaeval woods to the sober controversy of civilisation.' 'To outsiders, the position was not without its humour though the meeting was one of the most disorderly and unmannered I have attended for years', wrote the editor of the *Gazette*.

The meeting closed and the *Sussex Daily News* reported:

> the more excitable portion of the audience showed their feeling of resentment against the author of the scheme in a very marked manner. Mr. Prior was hissed and hooted as he left the Assembly Room and

on the way to his home in Tower Street, whither he was accompanied by the Superintendent of Police and other members of the force, he was followed by a yelling crowd who treated him to the same sort of battery of missiles which they normally reserved for the Salvation Army.

Eddis returned to London to report that the opposition was really not as strong 'as it would appear on the surface'. At least the meeting 'did a good deal in removing ignorance and mistaken views which were to a large extent due to misrepresentation, either wilful or undesigned, of interested people and personal opponents of Mr. Prior.' The immediate situation he felt was hopeless 'unless a new Secondary Education Act confers on the Commissioners additional powers of dealing with these Charities'.

However, within days of the inquiry there were signs of a change of heart. The Commissioners received letters of 'apology' from all classes of people who now urged their support. Among those who wrote was Robinson, editor of the *West Sussex Gazette*.

> The opposition you heard was directed against Mr Prior the man from motives inspired by his action on the drink problem. The suggestions he made are not objected to by Chichester's best men. Though they would doubtless prefer some other leader, they could not find one more genuinely able and inspiring. I sincerely hope for the sake of this desolate land that you will leave an open door for new action and give us a footing for further work.

The Trustees celebrated by buying new iron fencing for the school playground and closed their doors to day pupils for ever, and their minds to secondary education doing no more apart from acknowledging the Charity Commissioners' letter which stated that 'no alteration will take place in the school at present'. That chance, however, did not come again and the

7   Taken in 1897 outside Southgate House (site of the present County Court) on returning from the railway station having cheered the 'Volunteers' leaving for the Boer War. Mr Ballard wears a cocked hat of a Councillor. The uniform was probably not their best as only one boy is wearing the silver breast badge.

8   Ready for a game of cricket. Taken during the 1890s but the name of the Master is unknown.

City remained desolate of boys' secondary education until the opening of the Chichester High School for Boys in 1928.

As the pandemonium died away an uncomfortable calm returned to Chichester. Ballard went back to his cloistered existence and Oliver Whitby's School embarked upon a period of tranquillity. The Trustees continued to exercise their insular benevolence and, just as their predecessors had done, so now they, led by their Chairman Mr Smith, came 'and heard the boys recite, examined their drawings and heard them sing', and afterwards presented prizes, prayer books and bibles for leavers.

The Board of Education Act was passed in 1899 by which the powers of the Education Department, the Science and Art Department and the Charity Commissioners (in respect of those charities devoted to educational purposes) were merged into one body to be known as the Board of Education. Under the terms of the Act, the Board might 'inspect any school supplying secondary education and desiring to be so inspected, for the purposes of ascertaining the character of the teaching in the school and the nature of the provisions made for the teaching and health of the scholars.'

Clearly the Whitby School was not immediately involved nor affected since it was still able to pursue its path of independence. And although the Trustees had time and again acknowledged the force of law, they were equally certain of their position outside the law. At this time Mr Ballard decided to join the City Council and was made a member of the 'Technical Committee'. Both Greenwood and Eddis had expressed concern at the extraordinarily narrow curriculum of the school on the occasion of their visits in 1884 and 1891, and perhaps also as a result of the 1897 challenge to the academic position and worth of the school, Ballard now made certain token additions to the curriculum. Education at the

Whitby School could hardly have been called broad-based, but even Ballard may have become sensitive to the climate of opinion that expected more from an educated boy than mere perfection in handwriting. After all, these were the days when industry and commerce grew constantly, with competition for jobs becoming more severe. Ballard gained permission from the Trustees to allow the senior boys of the school to attend evening classes in shorthand, typing and book-keeping. They also authorised the payment of fees for boys to learn French at the Technical School.

National events, apart from education, made some small impact on the school. With the outbreak of the Boer War the boys listened to sermons in the Cathedral on the need for 'war relief', just as their forbears had done during the Crimean War. The boys joined other citizens in collecting books for the amusement of the 'soldiers during their leisure hours'. They marched to the railway station to cheer off the 'Volunteers' and, having been photographed with their Headmaster resplendent in the cocked hat of a Councillor, they were entertained to breakfast at Southgate House, the site now occupied by the County Court. Weekly they read letters 'sent home from the front' and during the Easter break of 1900 the school was used by the Middlesex Volunteers at a charge of 25 guineas per week. On 23 May the boys were woken at midnight by the pealing of the cathedral bells, and from their barred windows they saw and heard the crowds rejoicing at the relief of Mafeking.

As the new school year began in autumn 1900 that sense of financial security, which had fortified the Trustees in all their earlier brushes with authority, was showing signs of weakening; so great was their concern that they did not fill three vacancies. In fact, within twelve months they lowered the number of boys to thirty-six. According to the Trustees' Minutes between 28 March 1900 and 27 March 1901, 'it was ascertained that the expenses of the last 4 years had considerably exceeded the income.' This was apparently due to declining value of money, non-payment of rents and expenses on properties. Despite the financial constraints, boys continued to attend the Technical Institute whose prospectus at this time included such subjects as: 'Art, Geometry, Building Construction, Magnetism and Electricity, Physiography, French, Plumbing, Shorthand (Pitman), Ambulance (St John) and Nursing.'

The citizens of Chichester 'saw in' the year of 1901 by dancing around their fast decaying Market Cross. But within three weeks the cathedral bells rang out again; not this time in joy, but with a muffled peal proclaiming the death of Queen Victoria. As on all state occasions the 'Blue Coat Boys' paraded, their black arm bands in keeping with the yards of black crepe with which the cathedral and many other buildings were festooned for the Queen's memorial service.

During the first three years of the new century the government continued to debate education, realising the need for large-scale legislation but contenting itself with a number of temporary Acts. These only provided for the continuance of the existing state of affairs and made no provision for expansion. It became clear, however, that in the future the government would regard the local authority as the proper and competent authority for the organisation of secondary education and not the school boards.

The old problems surrounding the Oliver Whitby School again presented themselves. But this time there was a new antagonist, the West Sussex County Council, for the Chichester's school-board and attendance committee was no more, and Mr Ebenezer Prior's health was failing. Now was the very last chance to widen the scope and benefits of the school.

So, after two hundred years the Whitby School was again under scrutiny. The immediate chance to discuss the school's future came about through the Trustees' resolution that the old school buildings must be replaced.

Both Eddis and Greenwood had commented upon the poor state of the buildings but the Trustees had been disinclined to think of radical changes. Now they themselves sought permission to rebuild, and they came to the Board of Education as petitioners to spend some of their capital. However, the Board saw this as an opportunity to enforce some changes upon the school. No changes, no money. Having outlined their proposal for the erection of a new building, in a letter to the Board in August 1902, the Trustees suggested that the architect should be Reginald Blomfield and that the cost should not exceed £7,000.

Once more the Board requested information about the school, the qualifications of the staff, the curriculum and the timetable. The submission was prepared by Mr Ballard and still shows the continued placing of the school in two divisions and the same heavy emphasis on scripture and handwriting as in an earlier timetable. A Commissioner of the Board of Education, Mr G.B.M. Coore, came to Chichester on 17 November 1902 about the scheme to rebuild the school premises, on this occasion certain that he was in a better bargaining position than any of his predecessors had been in. He was met by Ballard, now aged 59, whom he found to be 'a man of strong personality and much concerned with his pension', and the Trustees who were still 'indifferent to the claims or needs of any secondary education in Chichester'. 'The opposition to any change was, however, qualified [Coore continued] by a sense of the dependence upon the Board in the matter of expenditure on new boarding house accommodation.'

The Commissioner, in his report, stressed the nature and history of the school. He commented that the inclusion of mathematics in a Blue Coat Boarding School founded in 1702 was certainly noteworthy, but there was little to raise the school above elementary level apart from the fact that some boys did shorthand and some did carpentry. He deplored the total lack of science teaching but was told by Ballard that 'the boys were not sufficiently advanced'. During discussions with the Trustees, Coore was told that they were 'not in favour of French' since it was 'useless', but they agreed to the introduction of Geometry and Elementary Science. The Trustees regarded the Birmingham Blue Coat School curriculum, which was put forward as a suggested blueprint, as 'too ambitious for Chichester'. Whereas Gardening and Carpentry received a favourable reception, Cookery was held to be singularly useless 'since few boys go to sea or enter the army'. Quite what the connection was, in their minds, we are not able to deduce.

The Board thought that the concept of a more representative government of 'voluntary' schools, provided for in the new Act, could be applied to Whitby's School but the Trustees, who had always proudly maintained their total independence in this matter, found the idea 'frankly distasteful'. However, they indicated that they might agree to a County representative; certainly not one from the Town Council, the thought of which was not merely distasteful but 'repugnant'. Coore comments: 'I was given privately to understand that the Chichester Town Council is held in low esteem by the class to which the Trustees belong.'

The Board was resolved to make changes to the Oliver Whitby School, but clearly had abandoned hope of making it a real secondary school. Prior and Robinson stressed to Coore in a confidential interview that no financial help could come from Chichester since 'it had reached its maximum borrowing due to the drainage scheme', and moreover 'its corporation did not give promise of sympathy for secondary education'. They were told of the proposal to divert some of the Whitby Capital towards the setting up of a secondary school in Chichester or towards providing secondary education. When this point was put to the Trustees, Coore writes, 'they did not flatly refuse to entertain it but they stated that the proposition was novel to them'. After much discussion the Trustees reconciled themselves to the idea of a Capital grant towards a secondary school provided that:

1) the Oliver Whitby boys could have 'free places';
2) there should be Church of England teaching;
3) the Trustees should provide a governor.

Back to London went Coore. His evidence and a new 'scheme' to replace that of 1826 were drafted and sent to the Trustees. In this the Board lowered the amount of capital expenditure to £6,000 and hoisted the Trustees with their own petard; they limited the boarding accommodation to 48 boys (the Trustees asked for room for 62 boys), having taken into account 'the special benefit claimed by the Trustees for the boarding system, viz. the personal supervision of the boys by the Head Master'. The Board stipulated three things upon which the building grant would be made: firstly, the curriculum must be broadened and the boys allowed to attend the Technical Schools or classes in Chichester; secondly, there must be local representation on the board of governors, one from the County and one from the City Council; thirdly, a capital sum of £1,500 must be given towards secondary education, the Board for its part accepting the terms outlined by the Trustees.

The Trustees miraculously, given their past record, agreed in general with the terms, although they bargained for £1,000 towards secondary education since 'due to broadening the curriculum and the need for another master' they could not afford more. On the question of representation they were adamant: they did not want a member of the Town Council especially if he were not Church of England, even though Eddis in London failed to see 'what the most rabid nonconformist could do amidst such a strong Church body'. Coore, for his part, was very worried that the 'conciliatory spirit' of the Trustees was in danger yet again of turning antagonistic. However, in a letter to the Trustees, Eddis, who knew them only too well, agreed to the figure of £1,000 but insisted on the 'Town Council' representative, who should be Church of England or the Mayor *ex-officio*. But for the Trustees the spectre of Ebenezer Prior, the nonconformist, reforming Mayor, was too real and so after a meeting they wrote informing the Board of Education that they would accept an elected representative from the Council provided he was a member of the Church of England.

During the summer of 1903, with a gesture of a new enlightenment the Trustees ordered that the iron bars on the windows of the school should be removed. Finally, after a number of curt reminders from the Trustees, a draft of the new scheme was sent from London 'for confidential consideration'. During the autumn the Trustees made final minor amendments, suffered the resignation of Mr Coombe Miller, who would not accept the altered scheme, and met finally on 9 January 1904 to 'take steps for publication'. Two days later passers-by in West Street could read a copy affixed to the door of the School House.

Prior was bitterly disappointed and West Wittering raised the old Snuggs' cry for special treatment. Both received scant satisfaction from the Board and less sympathy. The Board received a severe rebuke from the Headmaster of The Prebendal School, which had been considered as a suitable school to benefit from the Whitby Capital grant.

The Trustees, showing their independent spirit to the bitter end, acted and bought some land 'to straighten out their boundary wall' pending the rebuilding. Having always regarded themselves beyond the control of a central authority, they must have been amazed to receive a letter in which the Board regarded their action 'as a serious matter that the Governors should consider themselves at liberty to act without reference to us'.

There can never have been a more independent school. However, that fiercely protected independence would vanish, for on 26 October 1904 the scheme for the Oliver Whitby School was sealed and became law. It remained as the instrument of Government until the closing of the school.

9   The rebuilt premises of Oliver Whitby School in West Street, Chichester.

Five

Enlightenment to Decline and Fall
1905–1949

An uncertain calm had settled over Chichester and Oliver Whitby's School by the end of the first four years of the new century. Prior's cause had been lost. Ballard and the Governors, as they were now to be called (no longer Trustees of the Foundation as this responsibility had passed to the Board of Education through the instrument of Government), sat back on their laurels. The 'Great White Queen' had passed away and with her the Industrial Revolution which had given Britain an Empire, the aeroplane and the automobile.

The Governors moved ahead with the demolition of the old school, which had been extended and enlarged from time to time over the years but was now totally unsuitable for 20th-century expectations. They appointed Sir Reginald Blomfield as architect and chose to use a Chichester builder, Mr Vick, himself an Old Blue Coat Boy. Between them they erected a fine modern building on the same site. In addition to the imposing entrance and hall, there was a large dining hall and two floors of dormitories with ancillary bathroom and washrooms. From the hallway, looking out to West Street, the left-hand wing of the building was the Headmaster's residence, whilst the kitchens and other domestic rooms occupied the right wing. To the rear of this building were the playground, a school garden and a covered way to the old school rooms which bordered Tower Street. Rebuilding appears to have gone smoothly whilst the boys were put into temporary accommodation at 21 Tower Street. Roman pottery and coins were discovered during the digging of the foundations for the new building, together with cannon balls, presumably from the Civil War.

Mr Ballard was taken seriously ill in September 1906, soon after the new school building had been opened, and he retired in April 1908 on a pension of £120 per annum after 37 years as Headmaster and seven years as Assistant Master before that. In May of that year three Board of Education inspectors, Messrs Burrows, Swain and Dr Moffat, visited the school. They expressed themselves satisfied with everything they had seen and heard, but pleaded for a broadening of the curriculum to include science, woodwork and metal work.

There were 350 applicants for the post of Headmaster and, from a shortlist of 40, Charles Fairbrother from the Sir John Cass Foundation at Aldgate in London was appointed. He took up his post in August 1908 with a salary of £150 per annum plus board and lodging. After what might be regarded as the tyrannical years of Ballard one can imagine the apprehension of the 38 boys as they saw their new master for the first time. But Fairbrother was, by all accounts, a just man of sound educational views, cultured and with vision, under whom an era of enlightenment began. He abolished flogging and relaxed the oppressive

63

10   The School dining hall. Boys at mealtime with the Headmaster and Matron (Mr and Mrs Fairbrother) with the Head boys.

11   Classroom, Tower Street school building.

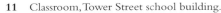

Note: Illustrations 10-18 were taken during the 1920s by an unknown photographer using glass plates. The plates are now in the care of Chichester District Museum, and this is almost certainly the first time they have been published.

12 The Headmaster's desk, Tower Street school building.

13 The School cricket team. We must presume the score, 271 for one wicket with the last man scoring 81, is correct!

14 & 15   Summer scout camp in the 1920s. These may well be different years in view of the change in location and also the attire of Mr Fairbrother (Headmaster).

16   *Above left.* A swimming party, probably at scout camp.

17   *Above right.* Proud 'Big Game Hunter' at scout camp.

18   *Right.* Mrs Fairbrother, Matron.

discipline of former years. He began a School Savings Bank and in 1910 started the 6th Chichester Boy Scout Troop at the school, which had the honour of being inspected by Lord Baden Powell, only two years after he had founded the Scout movement. According to one of Mr Fairbother's sons the visit took place during the school holidays and he remembered gathering together, within half an hour, as many of the boys as possible from around the City. It was, however, a memorable occasion.

Fairbrother realised that the Oliver Whitby School must compete within the new 'secondary' education system and, with the addition of a second assistant teacher, he was able to prepare boys for the 'Oxford Junior Examination'. During the first six years as Head-master, Fairbrother arranged for woodwork to be introduced as a lesson, a regular course of physical exercises, together with freehand drawing and science illustrated by experiments for which apparatus was provided. A report, following the annual visit by the Board of Education Examiner in December 1910, emphasises the benefits gained by the boys. 'The improved bearing of the lads is due largely to the attention to physical training'. The connection with 'the Boy Scouts movement is responsible for a great deal of the alertness shown by the elder lads'. The report further commented on the advantage of a broader curriculum and the nucleus of a school library. Fairbrother also improved material comforts with the installation of electric light and the introduction of central heating for the schoolrooms. Mr Ballard, who died on 26 March 1909, would have thought all this the height of pampering—only to be surpassed in 1914 by the provision of slippers for the boys! In the main, however, the daily routine for the boys and the school remained the same.

During the 1914–18 war the food was even plainer and boys commented that it was repetitive, but because of shortages one imagines that very little went to waste. As what today would be called an extra-curricular activity, members of the Scout Troop helped as messengers at the Military Hospital housed at Graylingwell. The Governors insured the School against damage by 'aircraft' and 'bombardment from the sea' and, to indicate what was to become crippling economic pressure, the costs per boy per day rose from 3s. 1d. in March 1914 to 4s. 0d. by June 1916. This cruel war caused tragic losses in the ranks of old boys, as it did to all schools throughout Britain.

After the war the customary pattern of life was resumed. By the early 1920s the Oliver Whitby School had restored its status as a 'higher' educational establishment, although no-one could decide what sort of school it was, being on 'the line between elementary, secondary and technical'. Generally speaking, it provided for the poorer classes among whom there was always the keenest competition for entry. Many Old Boys have recorded that, faced with a 'post elementary' education, the choice for them was between Midhurst Grammar School and Oliver Whitby's School, since Chichester had no Boys Secondary (Grammar) School until 1928.

Fairbrother's humanity was all pervading and those Old Boys who knew him testified to the warmth of his affection and sense of justice. It was a great shock, therefore, when he died suddenly in 1931 at the comparatively early age of fifty-two. His years as Headmaster are notable for two main things: firstly, his attempts to make the school rise out of the rut of 'charity' schooling; and secondly, his witness to steep rises in costs, of which the salary paid to an assistant master of £40 per annum in 1913 and £100 per annum in 1927 are symptomatic. (The School now had a 'fixed' income derived from capital stock assets.)

With effect from 1 September 1931 the last (and tenth) Headmaster, Horace A. Spendlove, was appointed, and Mrs Florence Spendlove, at the request of the Governors, was appointed Matron to the school. Under them the liberal traditions of Fairbrother were carried on and the curriculum was, over time, expanded to include additional subjects such as Shorthand, Foreign Languages, Algebra, Trigonometry and Higher Mathematics, required by senior boys who by 1939 would have to stay on at school until they were fifteen. Boys became more involved with the social life of Chichester with visits to art exhibitions, lantern slide lectures and watching films at the Plaza and Exchange Cinemas. Boys also took part in national celebrations in Priory Park, such as Empire Day and the Coronation of King George VI in 1937. Every summer a number of boys, together with the Headmaster and Matron, would go on a camping holiday, usually to the Isle of Wight.

During Spendlove's Headship the school materially prospered, notably by the addition to the buildings in 1938 of a fine gymnasium with a stage and woodwork/handicraft workshops built above, all finished off with a low garden wall for which the Chairman of Governors, Sir William Bird, gave two stone plant bowls to be placed on stone-capped pillars. Academically the school progressed with excellent results in the Oxford Local Examination. But Mr Spendlove and his wife lived with the ever increasing hazard of rising costs and a decreasing income. Then came the war of 1939-45. At times it became impossible to employ an assistant master and thus no boys were entered for the Oxford Examinations. Often the Headmaster and his wife did without domestic help, and 'made-do-and-mended'.

During the war, with no assistant teacher, Mr Spendlove became sole teacher to all 38 boys. This meant dividing his time between three classes, whilst Mrs Spendlove became cook and nursemaid. During those dark days

19 Mr Horace A. Spendlove, Headmaster, 1931-49.

20 Mrs Florence Spendlove, Matron, 1931-49.

21   For almost 250 years boys made this journey from the school to the Cathedral on Sundays. This picture was taken in 1932.

22   A group of boys in the playground, 1933.

23 Boys clearing debris after damage to the gymnasium and other school buildings by an enemy bomb during the Second World War.

the school suffered from enemy attack when during an air-raid on 10 February 1943 a 500kg bomb fell and, before exploding in Chapel Street where it demolished a number of houses with some loss of life, 'bounced' in the school garden, passed through the gymnasium causing serious destruction, and demolished the garage including Mr Spendlove's new car, a grey Lanchester, registration number AYO233. It also destroyed the garden potting shed and caused widespread superficial damage to the school building as all the windows were 'blown in'. Lessons were temporarily held in the dining room, whilst groups of boys were detailed to clear away the bricks, timber, glass and other debris. They had to clean all the bricks that could be salvaged ready for the builder to carry out the rebuilding work.

During the early part of the war, England was put on Double Summer Time and lessons started at the earlier time of seven o'clock in the morning with breakfast at seven-thirty; lessons recommenced at eight-thirty, finishing at lunchtime. The afternoons were used for 'prep' (preparation homework) and as soon as it grew dark the boys would have their tea and then proceed to bed, thus saving on light, heat and also ensuring some sleep, should it be necessary to wake the boys in case of air-raids and proceed to the cellar which acted conveniently as their wartime shelter.

So the war ended and the boys were allowed out from school to join in the City's celebrations in May 1945 to mark the end of the European conflict and, in August, on the capitulation of Japan. Horace Spendlove and his wife, whilst privately mourning the untimely deaths of young men they had cared for and taught, must have tempered their public rejoicing with a sense of foreboding, knowing, as they surely did, that the financial health

24 & 25 Annual Summer Camps resumed after the war in 1946. These photographs were probably taken in the New Forest on one of many sites the boys visited.

of the school was precarious if not terminal. Post-war running costs increased alarmingly, the effect and implications of Butler's Education Act of 1944 were as yet, unknown, and the attitude of a post-war Government to a private/state system of education was unclear. The Headmaster and Matron were likely to have reflected on the halcyon days of the Foundation. For example, in the 19th century 'The flourishing state of the finances of [the] Charity' enabled the Trustees 'To give a hundred pounds towards a schoolhouse being at this present time erected in the Parish of Birdham, an adjoining parish to West Wittering.' Likewise in the last quarter of the century the annual income appears to have averaged £2,000 and outgoings some £500. (This in today's 'real terms' approximates to £104,247 and £26,062 respectively).

Files covering the war and immediate post-war periods, however, do not indicate any imminent financial 'crisis' until the Clerk to the Governors (H.W. Symonds) wrote in October 1946 informing the aged Sir William Bird, Chairman of Governors, that the income for the year would be £1,907 and outgoings £1,802. Presumably things did not change radically until the early summer of 1949 when Symonds, again writing to Bird, told him that the 'balance at the bank is exhausted'. The clerk also says in his letter to his elderly Chairman that he has been instructed by the Governors to seek an overdraft of £1,000 and also to approach the County Council about the possibility of the school acting as a kind of hostel taking in 'boarders' from Chichester High School for Boys. But by 28 June 1949, after an approach to London, the Ministry of Education had indicated their objection to the raising of an overdraft and formally, it appears, recorded their refusal by letter at the end of July. Meanwhile on 11 July Colonel Richard Henty, head of the local firm of brewers (who by this time was the 'executive' Chairman with Sir William Bird in a 'titular' role), a fellow Governor Walter Stride, a prominent Cicestrian, and Symonds met the Chairman of West Sussex County Council, Major Eric Stanley Shaxson (Chairman of the County's Education Committee) and the Director of Education (Evan Davis) with his officers, Page and Cox, in attendance. The idea of providing some 20 boarding places as a Hostel for the Chichester High School was discussed but was not pursued, as the County Council was already making, as needed, provision for such boys who would attend, either at Midhurst or Steyning. Thus, only five days later, the Oliver Whitby Governors wrote to the Ministry of Education that the school was no longer viable and asking for help to prepare a scheme 'to retain the name, traditions and management of the school and its association with the Church of England, and, at the same time enable the school to perform a useful function in the present structure of national and local Education'. The Governors clearly hoped that representatives of the Ministry would visit Chichester to discuss any 'scheme'. Ironically, Whereas in 1897 a representative of the Board of Education, Eddis, had come to the Governors to discuss the Prior Scheme, now in August 1949 the Ministry of Education made it quite clear that it would not send a representative to Chichester but that a deputation from the Governors must go to London. So on 30 August Colonel Richard Henty, the Headmaster, Mr Spendlove and the Clerk to the Governors went to the Ministry.

Mr Spendlove, with justification, might have felt that without his and his wife's careful housekeeping the school's financial plight might have been worse. However, it could not have been music to the ears of the Chairman and Clerk to hear the Minister's representative's (Mr Hughes) opening statement that, 'seen from a legal and business aspect ... the objects of the Foundation had failed in consequence of the Governors' inability to carry on the

26 Mr Spendlove with
'Colonel' at the school playing
field, *c*.1946.

27 Mr Spendlove and the boys
at West Broyle, 1948.

school within the limits of the endowed income and the School should be closed forthwith.' At the meeting various suggestions were put forward and these included: parents paying towards the cost of maintenance; 'selling up' and providing for boys at, say, Christ's Hospital; the use of the buildings as a Youth Hostel; and the use of funds deriving from the sale for the support or setting up of a Church of England-aided School (or Schools). It was agreed that parents would be told that the School would close at Christmas 1949—and Colonel Henty went off to France until 16 September!

The news of the school's impending closure was received with dismay by the locality at large, by former pupils and the beneficiaries in the parishes of Harting and West Wittering together with Chichester itself. Meanwhile the Cathedral's Administrative Chapter at its meeting on 7 October heard from the Archdeacon of Chichester (Lancelot Mason) that the Governors of the Oliver Whitby School could no longer maintain the school and it was

28 The School's 1948 football team. Left to right, back row: Michael Elleker, Robin Hill, Peter Langley, John Messam, Peter Welch, Michael Hatcher; front row: Richard Doncaster, John Haffenden, Paul Langley, Dennis Aslett and Eric Burnand.

29 *Left.* Reg Courtney (1916–20) in his Sunday best gown.

30 *Above.* Twin brothers, John (Jack) and Frederick Hoskins (1922-8) in their Sunday best. From the period 1910 to 1934 ten members of this well-known West Wittering family attended the school. The addresses of the family were all in Coombes Row.

decided to consider ideas that might lead to a merger with The Prebendal School. The Chapter, with the Dean (A.S. Duncan-Jones) as Chairman, consisted of the Precentor (Canon Browne-Wilkinson), Provost of the Woodard Schools (Lancing *et alia*), Canon W.K. Lowther-Clarke (Librarian and renowned historian of the S.P.C.K. and its involvement with the Charity School Movement); Canon A. Powell (former Headmaster of Epsom College); Canon Walsh and Archdeacon Lancelot Mason. Such a group could reasonably be judged able to conduct a realistic and informed debate as to any possible future collaboration with the Cathedral's Prebendal School. To that end it was agreed that Browne-Wilkinson and Powell should have discussions with Henty and Stride, prepare a scheme and present it to the Chapter 'within the next three weeks'. Following the Chapter's meeting Archdeacon Mason wrote on 11 October a personal note in confidence to Walter Stride with a few ideas, no doubt deriving from the exchanges he had with his fellow Chapter members. So, while Browne-Wilkinson and Powell put their minds to proposals that were ultimately presented to their Chapter colleagues, Henty and Symonds, presumably with the agreement of the School Governors, went off to London on 14 October to discuss with the Clerk of Christ's Hospital (R.C. Evans) their hopes that places could be found for Oliver Whitby Boys at Horsham. A week later on 21 October, the Cathedral Chapter met, agreed a plan for some kind of 'marriage' of The Prebendal School with Oliver Whitby's School and duly sent this to Alderman Stride and his fellow Governors. On 28 October, the Governors of Oliver Whitby's met, decided 'to provide scholarships to Christ's Hospital' and, on the following day, wrote to Christ's Hospital's Clerk telling him of their resolve 'subject to Ministry of Education formal consent'. On the same day the Governors, in the person of the Clerk, wrote to the Chapter:

31 Mrs E. Marsh with her son (William) and grandson (Peter) who both attended the school. This photograph, taken in 1938, shows an example of the blazer, tie and pullover introduced in 1926.

32 John (Ricky) Haffenden and Robert (Bob) Ide wearing the battle-dress blouse introduced in the late 1930s.

33 The School closed on 12 December 1949. The Dean of Chichester (A.S. Duncan-Jones) shakes hands with each boy after a special service had been held in the cathedral.

'I am to state that the Governors are of the opinion that no useful purpose can be served by the continuance of any future discussion relative to any arrangement between The Prebendal and Oliver Whitby Schools.' There is no formal Chapter Record of the Dean and Chapter's reaction. However, Dean Duncan-Jones privately fulminated: 'What else could be expected of a group of retired Generals, superannuated Admirals, obsessed with those ridiculous blue gowns and presided over by a custard maker—Sir William Bird?' (The jibe about the school's historic costume might well be thought ironic coming from one who habitually appeared in public in buckled shoes, stockings, breeches, flared cassock and preaching tabs!)

As the discussions with Christ's Hospital forged ahead the Ministry of Education began to be anxious about the constitution of the Governing body under any proposed new scheme for the Charity, and stressed its view that the Oliver Whitby School was a 'Church' school. Symonds was asked by the Ministry whether or not the proposed plan had the support of the Chichester Diocesan Education Committee. As Clerk he replied that there had been 'informal discussions' with the Cathedral, but this, of course, was *not* the question that had been put! Moreover Symonds, possibly prompted by Admiral Phipps-Hornby, asked whether he had 'by statutory enactment or order' to tell the Diocese or 'merely as a matter of courtesy'. For good measure the 'Church' nature of the Oliver Whitby School was again challenged with the Ministry of Education by the Governors of the School.

New Year, 1950, dawned and the School had been closed. Part of the debate about the new Governing Body concerned suggestions by the Ministry that the Diocese should have *two* places; the one to be reserved for the Bishop (or his deputy) was producing a state of apoplexy among the Governors. The Ministry of Education was challenged by the Governors, who were no doubt amazed to learn that in June 1949 George Bell, the Bishop of Chichester, himself had been to London for discussions about the most appropriate use of the Whitby Foundation funds. The Ministry of Education felt they would not be 'justified' in giving way concerning Church representation, and the School Governors were equally 'adamant': 'there being absolutely no suggestion that he [Oliver Whitby] ever desired that one of the Governors [Trustees] must be a high functionary of the Church of England'; lest there be any misunderstanding, the idea was 'an innovation the Governors feel unable to accept in principle'. The Ministry was still batting, as it were, for the Bishop until a Ministry/Phipps-Hornby/ Symonds meeting on 23 June at which a powerful broadside was doubtless fired! During the next days and weeks, though the Ministry persisted in its view that the school was 'a strongly Church of England Foundation', discussions with the Diocese resulted in the peace-loving and anything-but-high-functionary Bishop Bell withdrawing 'his' claim to an *ex-officio* place on the Governing Board of the Oliver Whitby Foundation.

34   The Final Duty of the Governors, Headmaster, Matron and Assistant Master as they join the boys for a last photograph, 12 December 1949.

Chichester lost the chance of having a large Church of England Voluntary Aided School. So, for the second time, the Ebenezer Prior vision of 1897 was never fulfilled. Now, as even fewer benefit from a great and generous 300-year-old benefaction, some may have the sneaking thought that the highly successful Bishop Luffa Church of England School might well have carried the name and traditions of Oliver Whitby!

As we have seen, whenever the time for change was right the wrong men were at hand. Of no school can it more aptly be said that 'There is a tide in the affairs of men, which, taken at the flood, leads on to fortune'. The tide was in full flood in 1897, but from then on it was fast ebbing. Except by those boys who were given an invaluable start in life, Oliver Whitby's School may not be judged a great school. It set out with qualities that were by no means unique but not generally found. It conceded little to conventional educational thought and practice. It shielded itself from the contamination of the state system on the one hand and lacked vision to follow the example of other independent schools on the other.

That any school should survive for 250 years is noteworthy and that it should remain unchanged in character is remarkable. That it should have closed through lack of vision and because of personal animosities is tragic. To the end the School maintained its standard of discipline, good manners and emphasis on those qualities that are not measured by examination. From the first Headmaster, Robert Clarke, who served the school so faithfully up to the great years of the seemingly irascible C.R.H. Ballard (ironically nicknamed by the boys as *cherub*) to its final decades with Charles Fairbrother and Horace Spendlove, the Trustees together with the boys and their school were fortunate in the devotion of the Masters. In his sermon at the closing of the school the Dean of Chichester (A.S. Duncan-Jones) noted that there was significance in the very names of the last two Headmasters—Fairbrother and Spendlove. Had these liberal-minded men, both selfless in the extreme, been at the school in those crucial years of the 19th century the Oliver Whitby School might have still flourished today.

On the badges worn by every boy, as ordered by Oliver Whitby in his will, and, as a gift of Mrs Weller-Poley, carved in stone above the front door of the school (still there for everyone to see) is the Founder's motto *Vis et Sapientia*. Alas, where were strength and wisdom?

Six

Times Remembered

An Old Boy of 1945-49 writes:

On the evening of VE day, 8 May 1945, I cheered with the rest of the crowd as we literally danced around the giant bonfire which had been built in Chichester Cattle Market, just off Eastgate Square. To a small ten-year-old boy, the excitement was probably more to do with the opportunity to have fun and getting caught up in the occasion than really appreciating the significance of what it all meant. But I had other things on my mind, for in September I was to start five years at the Oliver Whitby School. So it was with trepidation that I watched the boys in their smart uniforms, who had been allowed out from this boarding school to celebrate with the other citizens of the City. I watched, anxious to ask one of them, any of them, 'What is it like at the school?' I really cannot remember how many I asked or their replies, but I know that as September grew closer so the anticipation mounted until the start of those days we call—The happiest days of our life.

We do not know how many boys attended the Oliver Whitby School throughout its almost two hundred and fifty years. For the first two hundred years there are virtually no records of the boys' observations during their time at the school. However, for the final fifty years a number of Old Boys have supplied reminiscences and accounts of their experiences at the school. This chapter attempts to capture (and frequently in their own words) some of their memories of people and events which had an influence on their lives, and where relevant their perception of those important never-to-be-forgotten schooldays.

It will always be appreciated that the Trustees' and Governors' best intentions were for the benefit of all the boys and of the school as a whole. During most of the life of the school, society was firmly of the opinion that 'children should be seen and not heard'. It is, therefore, no surprise that in the memories from Old Boys are frequent references to the fact that they were not made aware of the history or the day-to-day running of the school. They simply knew that Oliver Whitby was their benefactor, they were proud of him, appreciating what he had done for them. The boys rarely came into contact with the Trustees or Governors, except at inspections or on a special occasion such as prize-giving. Nevertheless, a few of them are remembered by name usually for their gifts to the school and one in particular was Sir William Bird (of Bird's Custard fame), who appears to have been more popular than most; he took a particular interest in cricket, often inviting boys to play in matches at Eartham, where he lived. Gifts from the Trustees and by Governors were not always that attractive, ranging as they did from a new electric glue pot, for woodwork, to in 1932, a G.E.C. Wireless set or, on a number of occasions, cricket equipment. In 1938 a new piano was presented to the school, which may well have been a replacement for the harmonium bought in the 1870s. Admiral Phipps-Hornby took particular interest in the library and presented a quantity of books on a number of occasions. Sporting opportunities were greatly increased when, in 1926, as a memorial to his father, Thomas Weller-Poley JP, of West Broyle, who had been a Governor of the school for 29 years, and Chairman for 21 of them, Captain E.H. Weller-Poley purchased and gave to the school the sports and playing field which was situated where Sherborne Road, Parklands, is now.

Little detail is known of the school's earlier staff, with the exception that Headmaster W. Wheatley (1808) may have proved unsatisfactory and T. Pescod (1841) was not well treated upon his retirement. There are more details from the time of Charles Ballard which are recalled by Old Boys. Ballard was, without doubt, a hard disciplinarian; punishment was both frequent and severe, but he had a positive human touch as well. When Ballard was employed as Assistant Master and following Pescod's severe illness when boys acted as 'monitors' (probably in a 'pupil teacher role'), he arranged for each boy to be paid 10s. in recognition of his service! Ballard was proud of the school and the boys he taught and frequently used mottoes to encourage his pupils: 'Train up the child the way he should go' and 'Anything worth doing is worth doing well' were two of his favourites. He was well respected by the boys, who nicknamed him 'Cherub', reflecting his initials, Ch. R.B. He had pet dislikes such as untidiness and his encouragement of smart penmanship is perhaps a reflection of this. Another obsession was dirt, 'stale dirt', as he persisted in calling it. It is said that in all copies of the text book, *English History*, where the Great Plague was attributed to dirt, he had boys insert the word 'stale'. Perhaps trying to excuse their Master's irascible behaviour, boys were said to dread the days he shaved and trimmed his beard, 'for on those days he seemed to have a wild temper'. It would have been quite enlightening if we only knew what Ballard's son, who joined the school in 1899, made of it all.

Charles B. Fairbrother's appointment in 1908 was surely a welcome change and there was a slow transition from the spartan life and intemperate behaviour. On his arrival at the school he was surprised to find boys cringing away from him and immediately abolished flogging.

Boys who experienced this transition confirm that he still expected high standards of cleanliness and discipline but fairness was the new ingredient. He was never hasty in his judgement. He would also use dictums, such as 'Locked in our heads' when referring to 'remembering', and 'The speed of the class is the pace of the slowest boy' used as encouragement to the slower learners to keep up with their peers. A great sportsman, he taught his boys to 'Play hard, play to win, but above all play the game'.

We know that Ballard, so affronted by the heresies, as he saw them, preached in the Cathedral, had no compunction in storming out in the middle of sermons. So also Fairbrother had his own way of showing impatience at the length of sermons: he would lay out a line of sixpenny pieces and remove one every five minutes of the sermon. Any left were placed in the collection plate.

Many of the Old Boys who passed through the school during his 23-year headship have commented on his personal interest in his pupils, which extended beyond their time at school for he would help them to find work. He often went with the boys to visit the local hospital, factories and offices. He died suddenly at the relatively young age of 52, and we can imagine how deeply saddened the boys would have been.

Horace A. Spendlove, the last Headmaster, was appointed in 1931, an imposing figure with military bearing and a dapper white moustache. He was always immaculate, well

35   The Sick Bay with patient, *c.*1920.

groomed and expected the boys to be similarly turned out. It is said that, coming from Derby, he was not too keen on the boys' Sussex accents. The more liberal approach to discipline introduced by Fairbrother was continued under Spendlove, but it would be wrong to think of his regime as anything but authoritarian. When the occasion demanded, he was quite capable of administering the most painful corporal punishment to defaulters. Few boys would have escaped a clip around the ear or a painful tap on the head with his stubby 'music stick'. Perhaps his most painful 'encouragement' was to lift boys from their seats with a pinch of their hair firmly held between his forefinger and thumb. Timid nine-year-old waifs were, at first, afraid of him but later came to revere and respect him. Boys say that they can never recall him laughing, but some consider themselves privileged to have witnessed him smile on a number of occasions. He was an extraordinary man and, though many boys regarded him with awe, his firm but fair regime was beneficial and appreciated by all of his pupils.

Over the years the school employed a number of Housekeepers, part of whose duties was to monitor the welfare of the boys. Not many details are available of the bond there would have been between the boys and their Housekeeper. Mrs Vick was Matron for quite some time during Mr Pescod's headship, and was given notice to vacate 'the cottage' (this would be the schoolhouse at 52 Tower Street) of which Mr Ballard, as Assistant Master, was given rent-free use. In 1906 Miss Pakeman was appointed Matron and in December that year she made an appeal to the Trustees to be allowed £1 per quarter beer money. This was granted, making her salary £44 p.a.—including the beer money! When Fairbrother and Spendlove were Headmasters their wives were employed as Matrons.

Mrs Fairbrother was said to be strict but sympathetic. We are told by more than one boy that she 'had a standard white medicine for all minor ills', it tasted horrible and queuing for it was like a punishment in itself. This was probably a deliberate ploy to deter malingerers. One of Matron's duties was to carry out a weekly inspection of the boys' beds and she had a 'real obsession for finding the odd flea in any bed', so we are told.

Mrs Spendlove was a particularly popular Matron, Many boys talk of her as their matriarch, confidante and their confessor. It is said that, unless she was cross with some foolhardy boy, she always wore a smile. During the difficult years of the Second World War when cooks and kitchen staff were not readily available, being required in factories or at home to look after brothers and sisters while mother went to work, Mrs Spendlove found herself acting as the cook and general kitchen domestic. Not only would she prepare the meals but she also served the food to the boys. It was Matron's duty also to monitor the boys' hygiene, and supervise the weekly bath night. She was said to carry out all those tasks unselfishly, just as any mother would do for her children. There were three Spendlove children: Roy, who after some time in the Home Guard joined the army in 1942 on a weekly pay of 1s. 6d. and served in India; Hugh, who was an art student; and Freda who helped her mother and was a friend to many boys who had the misfortune to be taken ill, particularly if they were forced to spend time in the 'sick room'. One boy tells us that, when he was isolated with glandular fever, Hugh encouraged him to draw, supplying art materials and showing examples of his own work, whilst Freda loaned books, together with the luxury of a gramophone and records. This kindness assured many boys a speedy recovery and has never been forgotten. It is almost certain that less sympathy would have been offered to boys laid low in the Sick Bay during the epidemics of the 18th century including typhoid, smallpox, measles and something called 'the itch' which occurred at regular intervals. Even as late as 1893 the school suffered an epidemic of scarlet fever. However, we know that inoculation against more serious diseases, a major breakthrough in medicine during the middle of the 18th century, was used for boys at Oliver Whitby's as early as 1782.

Assistant Masters were employed in the school from the time when Henry Pescod's son, Thomas, assisted until he himself took over the headship. In turn he employed Charles Ballard in this post until he too became Headmaster. During the last forty years or so there was quite a number of Assistant Masters, many of whose names, for whatever reason, are lost to us. However, boys do recall some names, such as Mr J.D. Harris, taken on as 'second Assistant Master at a salary of £40 per annum including beer money, with board and residence during term time'. There was also Mr Bloomfield in 1912, who appears to have been very popular with a number of boys who remember him as strict though his encouragement in sport and his inspirational teaching method more than compensated for this. Mr Banks joined the school in 1914 as teacher of the junior classes.

After the First World War there was a succession of Assistants Teachers, Petter, Morgan, Mant and Mckay, but we know nothing of them beyond their names. In 1930 there was a Mr Pound, remembered as 'a jolly man and constant pipe smoker', but perhaps in the school's later days the two most popular were Mr Joe Ansell (1928), remembered for his competent singing voice and as an active member of the Chichester Operatic Society, whose perform-ances boys would often attend at the Exchange Theatre; and Mr Harry Snailham, appointed in 1931 on a salary of £100. Apart from being 'called up' for service in the Second World War, he worked under Spendlove, leaving only just before the school closed. Harry Snailham, nicknamed 'Bisto' in his early days at the school, appears from the affection shown by Old Boys to have been successful at gaining the confidence of pupils and, besides teaching academic subjects, was also involved with sport and physical education, although after the gymnasium had been built in 1938, a number of temporary gymnastic instructors was employed. From the Trustees' Minute Book we learn that in the 18th and 19th centuries a number of Underservants was employed. There are no records of their names, but there is mention of their being replaced for misbehaviour or, as in 1906, asking for wages during their holidays—1s. 0d. per day was granted to them during the time they were away from the school, when services were not required. Over the years several of the boys' sisters were employed in the positions of housemaid and cook, including Marjorie Ayling and her sister, Louise, taken on as a cook, at the end of the war in 1944. There are numerous references to kitchen staff being dismissed as 'unsatisfactory' and perhaps it was prudent that their names were not recorded. During the Headship of Charles Ballard, the 1901 census shows us that he not only lived at the school with his wife, daughter and son, but his sister also lived with them and was the school's 'sick nurse'.

During the late 1920s Mr T.H. Vickers is frequently mentioned; he was one of His Majesty's Inspectors, who carried out the annual official inspection of the school on behalf of the Board of Education. Nicknamed 'Daddy' for no reason that can be traced, apparently his singing of selections from *Messiah,* by Handel, was held in awe. Vickers was still making his annual visits in 1938-39, when he also carried out the more pleasant duty of making presentations at prize-giving.

Of the original 1712 building, details come only from the Trustees' accounts. These refer to general repairs, re-glazing of windows and the replacing of gas lighting in 1871. However, in 1738 there is a reference to the 'mending of the Pigeon House'; could this have been a source of fresh meat for the boys? Pigeons were a prime source of meat in many middle- and upper-class houses during the early part of the 18th century, as can be seen from the preserved beautiful dovecotes of those days. In 1745 we learn that there was refurbishment to the 'paving [in] the wash house'. The water supply was from a well and it was not until 1880, when the 'well water' was 'pronounced bad' by the Officer of Health, that Ballard was instructed to find out the 'annual charge for laying of water by the Chichester Water Company'. One of the last important jobs to the old building was the removal in 1903 of the iron bars from the upstairs bedroom windows and the fixture of a piece of rope nearby. This was the first attempt at fire safety, when, in a case of fire, the boys would climb down the rope to escape.

The new school building opened at the beginning of the school year in September 1906. It appears, from the Minutes of the Trustees of 24 April, that the boys' return from Summer Holiday was delayed to ensure that all the work was complete. It was built by an Old Boy (Messrs Vick and Sons) at a cost of £6,987 8s. 0d. The main building of the school complex was three storeys high, consisting of the dining hall, kitchens and washrooms on the ground floor with three dormitories each on two floors. There was a covered way linking it to the classrooms, still in a building of 18th-century origin, comprising a large downstairs recreation area, which served as a 'play-ground' during inclement weather. The upstairs was a large single classroom that could be divided to cater for the different levels of classes, with a wide wooden staircase joining these two floors. All the floors were un-carpeted and several times a day up to forty pairs of thundering feet would

36 Freehand drawing, by Arthur Groundsell whilst at the school, 1926-31, of the entrance to the main school building in West Street.

37   Group of boys in front of the gymnasium, 1946.

run up and down those bare wooden stairs oblivious to the noise they created. In retrospect one cannot help thinking of the people living next door in the house, also owned by the Oliver Whitby Foundation, which in years past had been home to Assistant Masters, House-keepers, Cooks and other staff.

In the recreation room there was a huge double door leading outside into Tower Street—this was the gateway to freedom! It was kept securely locked except when the boys were herded out into the street to line up and march, either for Cathedral services, the playing fields near Fishbourne, or the ritual Sunday afternoon walks. Most important of all, it witnessed the dash to freedom at the start of school holidays. However, it was also, of course, the entrance through which the boys reluctantly returned for the start of term. Ironically, the boys could hear the very audible sounds of life emanating from the outside world, but, as the windows in this school building were set so high, they could see none of it.

The third building, built in 1938, was the magnificent gymnasium with an integral stage at one end. It was severely damaged and then repaired during the Second World War, and was probably the most modern gymnasium of its type for many miles around. Fitted out with climbing frames, ropes and physical training apparatus, it was popular with most boys, although there were those, as in every school, who just did not like physical exercise. One element none of the boys appreciated was the gymnasium's specially oiled parquet floor— not only did this mean trouble if anybody walked on it without wearing plimsolls, but boys had to carry out the re-oiling and polishing. Above the gymnasium was a purpose-built woodwork and craft workshop. The whole building was covered in a beautiful Virginia creeper, at its most memorable in autumn when the brilliant red leaves were a mass of colour.

The boundary of these buildings enclosed an outside toilet and a covered workshop, where the boys' shoes were repaired or re-studded by one of the senior boys. This whole area was the tarmacadamed playground. We know that over the years a beautiful lime tree, which stood to one side of this area, served as an important feature in many school games; it could also be a place of solace on occasions when a boy wanted to be alone.

Within the walkway between the buildings was a series of 40 'pigeon holes' where boys were able to keep personal possessions. Each boy was given a number when he joined the school—one to twenty, Eagle House; twenty-one to forty, Falcon House. (Before 1931 the Houses had been called the Gordon and Wellington.) A member of a House Team could earn points for both schoolwork and sporting activities, and prizes and House Shields were awarded at the end of term. In 1900 due to the 'expenses of the last four years [having] considerably exceeded the income' the number of boys at the school was reduced again and in 1901 the number was lowered to 36 boys. There was an increase to 40 boys during the 1930s and '40s, but the maximum number of boys ever to attend the school was 52, in 1878.

The uniform at the school's inception was supplied, according to the accounts, by 'Mr. Parker in London', and consisted of a white long-tailed shirt to which the boys attached a collar, underneath which was buttoned what can best be described as 'Priests Tabs'. These lay over a navy blue waistcoat fastened by brass buttons up to the neck. The boys wore knee-length black stockings and navy blue breeches with three brass buttons which were fastened just below the knee. Over these was worn an ankle-length navy blue gown, lined on the upper half with a gold-coloured serge. This gown had brass buttons from neck to waist, but only the two lower buttons were done-up and a leather girdle was fastened around the waist between these buttons. It was to this gown that, in 1738, the breast badges—or 'the plates' as they are called in the accounts—were fixed— a silver badge for the Sunday gowns and

38 *Above left.* Head boy, *c.*1920s.

39 *Above right.* New boy in his Sunday best, date unknown.

'white metal' for other days. There are references in the accounts for 1830 and 1839 to the purchase of badges from Joshua Storrs of London: eight badges costing £10 0s. 0d. and six costing £7 10s. 0d. respectively, but whether these were silver or white metal we have no way of telling. With this uniform was worn an apprentice's hat of woven cotton with a strengthened full-circle brim and a bobble or 'tassel' on the crown. This was probably the uniform worn at all times up to 1926, although at some point the school started to use a local supplier, Messrs Bridger of East Street. The uniform proved very warm in winter and in summer the gown was left off except on 'high days' and Sundays. Boys recall that the breeches were very restrictive when playing football and other sport; tradition has it that football was played in gowns, with the 'skirt' being tucked into the girdle. Night-shirts and under garments were issued to boys on arrival at the school and one of their first jobs was to sew Cash's name tapes onto every article of clothing and of the uniform. This tested the dexterity and patience of all boys, many a tear being shed when an 11-year-old's sewing skills did not meet the Headmaster's requirement at the first attempt.

In 1926 a radical change was made to the daily uniform: for everyday wear, grey short trousers were introduced with grey blazers, ties and peaked caps, with a badge sewn onto the blazer breast pocket. The traditional gowns and breeches were still worn on Sundays and special occasions. Also at this time football 'togs' were introduced and cricket whites for boys playing in the best team. Otherwise white shorts and tops were worn for physical exercises. This attempt to modernise the uniform was too plain and in 1936 a far more distinctive and fashionable uniform was introduced: blue shorts and a blue battle-dress blouse were to be worn with the more traditional hat (without the brim and bobble); it was more like a beret and had for the first time a two-inch metal hat badge. The distinctive 'Priest Tabs' were to be worn with this day-to-day uniform. No change was made made to the traditional Sunday-best uniform of gown and breeches.

Available evidence reveals little change in the overall routine of the school from inception to closure, with only minor shifts in times and duties over the years. The day started at 6.30 a.m., and this changed to 7 a.m. during the latter years, when a hand bell was rung by the Bellboy who would have been woken by a Master or the Housekeeper. The bell would be rung outside the dormitories. When the boys rose they would strip their beds before going for a cold wash, returning to dress and make their beds. The cold wash, every morning, was a significant feature of the school throughout its whole existence. Sometimes washing was impossible due to the water 'freezing in the washbowl'. There would be a daily inspection of the dormitory by either the Headmaster, Matron Head Boy, or a Charge boy, ensuring that the beds were made up correctly and that nobody was staying in bed. We know that in earlier days boys attended some form of 'lessons' from 7-7.30 a.m., which may have been only prayers or reading the collect for the day. Breakfast followed. At 8 a.m. all boys would carry out their prescribed 'duties'. These jobs ranged from polishing brass door knobs and light switches to cleaning out the washroom. and polishing floors. Boys would also help in the kitchen by preparing vegetables. Others had more exciting jobs such as polishing the great oak staircase or the dormitory corridors. This latter task involved the boys becoming experts at handling a heavy polisher, known as a 'Ronuker'—the art was to hold onto the handle and swing it from front to back. However, this 'art' also became an unofficial 'sport', where two boys tried to beat each other by sending the polisher at great speed down a corridor without touching the side walls!

40 The Oliver Whitby memorial stone, which is on the wall above the family vault in the south cloister of Chichester Cathedral.

41 The Oliver Whitby stained-glass window in the north aisle of Chichester Cathedral was designed and installed not long before the school closed. One of the scholars, Ralph Lawrence, modelled for the artist's representation of a Blue Coat Boy.

We also know that the Oliver Whitby memorial in the Cathedral cloisters was, on occasions during the earlier years, cleaned by the boys. This was probably done each year before the anniversary of the Founder's death, 19 February, when a service was held in front of the memorial. But in 1823 it was necessary for a more professional job and James Stuart was paid £2 15s. 9d. for cleaning it. In 1889, however, a G. Knight was only paid £2 8s. 0d. for carrying out the same work.

To the boys, one of the more notable improvements was central heating, installed in 1929, and hot water pipes wended their way throughout the new building. However, hot water was still not generally available in the washrooms. This luxury would now be on tap for baths on Friday nights, and senior boys were responsible for looking after a separate boiler, lit for the purpose. Headmaster Ballard made an iniquitous rule that no more than five cinders, each the size of a pea, were allowed to fall into the ash tray. Once this rule was broken the boy responsible did not have food for two days! There were only two bath tubs, both in the same room, two boys taking a bath at a time, and each allowed ten minutes in the bath and two minutes to dry and get dressed. The next boys would undress while the last boys were dressing, so the conveyor-belt system got through the whole school of 40 boys within four hours. A senior boy, or 'Charge boy', sat on a wooden stool monitoring the proceedings, with the occasional visit from Matron or Headmaster.

42   The oak staircase, well known to every Blue Coat Boy who either polished the banisters or stood beside them in trepidation waiting outside the Headmaster's office. They can still be seen as part of the Army & Navy Department Store, West Street.

Cleanliness, as we know from Ballards' days, was always an important criterion. The morning inspection by the Headmaster paid particular attention to dress, hands, fingernails, and 'behind the ears'. Shoes were to be highly polished and, most important of all, they had to have all their studs. This fundamental experience was appreciated by many boys in later years when they found themselves joining the armed services. We have no early details of the school's arrangements for laundry, but during the last 150 years this was the responsibility of the boys' parents or guardians. In the early part of the 19th century boys went home for Saturday evenings taking their washing with them and collected clean clothes. The luxury of going home was stopped some time in the early 1800s, firstly to dissuade truancy and secondly to avoid boys catching and bringing back to school some prevalent disease such as typhoid, measles or smallpox. The new system meant that parents came to the school to collect the washing in a green bag, which became a familiar sight around Chichester on Saturdays. However, in the last 20 years of the school's existence, the colour of the bag was changed to white and the boy's name was stencilled across the front of it. Parents visited the school on Saturday afternoons, while the boys were away at the sports field. An important feature for the boys was that parents were allowed to leave special treats for them, such as sweets, fruit, jars of jam and Shippam's pastes, together with the all-important comics, which had just started to be published at this time.

What of the lessons, the classroom work, the curriculum? The Founder made it clear in his will:

> the said Master shall have for his teaching and instructing the said twelve boys, over and besides his lodging and diet in the said School House the clear yearly sum of twenty pounds per annum paid him by quarterly payments without any deduction for which he shall teach and instruct the said twelve boys in writing, arithmetic, and in the mathematics.

This was very much in line with many other charity schools in existence throughout Queen Anne's Britain. It was not until the 19th century that we find a wider curriculum. From time to time navigation was included, and also metrication and geometry; later algebra became part of the curriculum. Writing, or rather penmanship, was always of paramount importance and never more so than during Ballard's headship, for whom it was an obsession. In 1897, some boys gained the impression that good handwriting was the most important objective. Hours were spent perfecting their hand, when 'round hand' and ornamental lettering, probably calligraphy, were taught. Before examinations the penmanship of past years was often shown as an example of work required. However, by the end of the 1880s, writing constituted only one element of 'English' as a subject, which also included reading, dictation, grammar, spelling, composition and general literature. An inspector's report for 1870 stated that 'a Compound Sentence was parsed with tolerable accuracy', showing the high level of work now being achieved. The following table of subjects analysis shows how, over the last 70 years, time was spent on specific subjects, together with changes in emphasis on each subject:

General subject analysis by hours worked per week

Subject	1880	1912	1936
Scripture	$4\frac{5}{6}$	$2\frac{1}{2}$	$3\frac{1}{3}$
Mathematics	$6\frac{1}{6}$	$5\frac{2}{3}$	$6\frac{1}{3}$
English	$11\frac{1}{3}$	$9\frac{2}{3}$	$7\frac{2}{3}$
Geography	$4\frac{1}{6}$	$2\frac{1}{6}$	$2\frac{1}{6}$
History	$1\frac{2}{3}$	3	$1\frac{2}{3}$
Drawing	$1\frac{1}{3}$	2	$1\frac{1}{3}$
Music	$1\frac{1}{2}$	$2\frac{1}{6}$	$1\frac{1}{2}$
Cypher	$3\frac{1}{6}$	—	—
Examination	$1\frac{1}{3}$	$2\frac{2}{3}$	Subjects tested in Subject time
Physical Training	—	$\frac{2}{3}$	1
Science	—	1	$1\frac{1}{6}$
Gardening	—	$2\frac{1}{2}$	$1\frac{1}{3}$
Shorthand	—	$1\frac{1}{3}$	$\frac{5}{6}$
Hygiene	—	—	$\frac{1}{3}$
Handwork	—	—	2
Total Hours	**$35\frac{1}{2}$**	**$35\frac{1}{2}$**	**$30\frac{2}{3}$**

(Prepared by H.A. Spendlove, 1936)

Article 10 of the Trustees' original 1712 'rules', although obscure in its wording, was clear that examination of the boys' work was to be regular and open to all, including the public, who could visit the school on Sunday evenings and carry out an inspection. The spirit of this directive contined until the day the school closed, although the latest recorded examination to which the public were invited was in 1867, where 'style of reading' and 'neatness and accuracy of their slate work' were put forward for scrutiny. Examinations and inspections by H. M. Inspectors, who were now the people's representatives, are well documented. Whatever the sophistication of today's classroom appraisals, the constant monitoring of the boys' work over the 250-year life of the school ensured that Oliver Whitby Boys maintained a standard of excellence equal to the best of the day.

The Cathedral was very important in the life of the Oliver Whitby boys, while the teaching of scripture and also church music formed an integral part of the boys' experience. From 1712 right up to the First World War the boys attended church, either in the Cathedral or (at times after 1859) St Peter's, on both Sunday mornings and afternoons. In 1880 almost five hours a week was spent on scripture as a subject. The Collect for each Sunday was, as we know, learned by heart, and a boy was chosen to recite it before going to church. It is probably right to presume that much of the time recorded as 'being taught music' would in fact be spent learning hymns and other religious music. In 1916 elementary music was taught and it is on record that some boys practised campanology, with a complete set of handbells.

As the years passed, so exercise, sport and leisure became part of routine. It would be unwise to believe that, because the Trustees of the 18th century left no record of any leisure activities, none took place. Any group of 12 boys, within a small space, would have devised some form of games. These may have been rather crude forms of tag, wrestling or rounders, which was played in England from Tudor times, or even cricket, as the earliest recorded match was played in Sussex in 1697. The rudimentary raw material of the game of football was also to be found, although primarily in the fields and streets, among farm boys and apprentices. At this time, it was a folk game belonging to the people, but in the eyes of authority and the well-bred it was considered a vulgar and rowdy pastime. The respectable and the Godly observed it with distaste—it kept men from their Christian duties. It may be significant that not until 1862 do we find the Trustees committing to '2 years rent of a meadow [at] £4 0s. 0d., for cricket and exercise ground' from 'Mr Charles Chitty'.

By March 1904, the playing field was 'unsatisfactory'. Whether this was Mr Chitty's field we do not know, but in May of the same year we read that the 'Cricket field [was] rolled with a heavy roller and will do for the present'. However, by November things were getting serious and the School leased from a Trustee, Arthur Henty (Chairman of Henty's Brewery), a new playing field 'behind the brewery'. This arrangement, as far as we know, remained in place until the generous gift of the School's own playing field in 1926 by a Governor, Thomas Weller-Poley. We know that the playing field did have a groundsman, but only one name has been traced, that of Mr Shiers, a former Old Boy of the school. However, Mr Spendlove would use the boys to help maintain it. There are memories of trees and hedges being ruthlessly cut back, and of boys being lined up and made to kneel and to proceed in a row weeding the whole length of the playing area. One pleasurable duty, performed by either the Head Boy or a boy who achieved a special privilege was (instead of marching to the playing field on Saturday) to collect 'Colonel', a huge Clydesdale horse, from Dell Quay, and either ride or lead him to the playing field where Mr Spendlove would hitch on the mower or roller. Another boy would usually return the horse.

There is no doubt that attention was given to competitive sport over these years, and by 1905 the School was regularly playing both cricket and football. There were two teams: 'Chichester Town' representing City boys and 'Country' representing Wittering and Harting boys. There were regular matches played against both the Lancastrian and Prebendal Schools. Old Boys remember athletics meetings, or 'field and track sporting events' as they refer to them, being held in summer. Parents were very occasionally invited to these events, particularly when they involved visiting schools. Many boys recall the day in 1947 when 'Cossy' Page broke the record for throwing the cricket ball by such a margin that it was doubtful if anyone would ever beat him.

In the school recreation room, indoor games featured; skittles was popular in the 1920s along with table tennis, or 'Ping Pong' as it was then known. Board games were prolific and even card games were played, although these would almost certainly not have been permitted until well into the 20th century.

References have been made to the boys being taken on educational visits to local factories, including the tannery and Shippam's meat and fish paste manufacturer. They were often taken on journeys which filled them with great excitement. In 1872 was the first recorded train journey to the Crystal Palace. The fare 'by excursion train' for 'boys, Master, Matron and Servant as a holiday and treat' was quoted as £6 18s. 9d. This outing was repeated in 1873 and every other year until 1879. In 1880 they visited the 'Zoological Gardens' and in subsequent years went to 'Brighton' and 'London', and these outings were repeated during the 1890s. In June 1893 the boys were 'given a treat' to celebrate the marriage of the Duke of York and Princess Mary (King George V and Queen Mary). Most royal occasions warranted some form of celebration that involved the public and the boys at Oliver Whitby's were, it appears, always involved, for example by being included in processions through the City, as on Tuesday 22 June 1897, for the celebration of Queen Victoria's Diamond Jubilee. A procession to the Cathedral for the 11.00 a.m. service consisted of: THE BAND, THE MACE, MAYOR AND CORPORATION, CIVIC DIGNITARIES ETC., THE FIRE BRIGADE IN UNIFORM, THE CHICHESTER CYCLING CLUB, THE BOYS OF THE WHITBY SCHOOL, THE CHICHESTER FIFE AND DRUM BAND followed by 11 'Friendly Societies'. We cannot be certain whether the Oliver Whitby Boys attended the 'party' held in Priory Park during the afternoon, where there were sports and 'fire balloons—sent up at intervals', along with 2,000 children who had tea, and also received a Jubilee mug.

Throughout the last 50 years of the school outings to London and Brighton continued, but also more local entertainment became possible with the advent of the cinema. Boys remember visits to the cinema with a fondness for particular films, *Vice Versa*, *The Guinea Pig*, *Oliver Twist* starring John Howard Davies as Oliver, and also T*om Brown's Schooldays*. There were also annual visits to the Exchange Theatre (this theatre became the Exchange Cinema and is currently a McDonald's), where the boys watched the Chichester Operatic Society in performances of Gilbert and Sullivan's operettas. Other activities included a jazz band (1926) and of course the scout troop. After the war, in 1946 and in subsequent years, Mr and Mrs Spendlove would take a number of boys camping on the Isle of Wight. This was a very popular holiday, and the boys received pocket money from the Governors to spend on sweets, cakes and toys.

It is not certain when the mandatory Sunday afternoon walk started, but during Mr Spendlove's headship it became established routine. The boys would march smartly two abreast whilst within the City Walls. They were always admired by the citizens of Chichester who often remarked on their neatness and precision. Once outside the City limits the boys could break ranks and walk casually. The routes taken were variously across Westgate Fields and on to Dell Quay or Bosham, Chichester Harbour, Lavant and other villages in Sussex. Not only was the freedom appreciated by the boys but very often it proved to be an introduction to nature with Mr Spendlove, in particular, providing the names of birds, trees and plant life.

If the Sunday walk provided a welcome to liberty, it was no match for the boys' favourite recreation, the regular summer visits to The Broyle. This was the private estate of one of the Governors, Captain Weller-Poley. Here, out of sight of any authority, the boys were able to run wild in what to them must have seemed like a forest. They could climb trees, play cowboys and Indians, or exercise their wildest imaginations from their temporary dens. Some of the boys remember smoking vines, thin ones for beginners and thick ones, like 'cigars', for the older boys, unperturbed that many were made ill by the experience. During spring and summer more purposeful visits were made to The Broyle when a number of boys were taken to 'dead head' the rhododendrons, something about which Mrs Weller-Poley appears to have been fanatical.

43 Boys sitting on the school garden wall—Welch, Philmore and Haffenden.

Other leisure activities which can only be described as extra-curricular—occasions when boys simply took the situation into their own hands, performing daring, risky and forbidden pursuits without being caught; or so they hoped. Mostly these were carried out during the long dark winter evenings and had to be completed before 8.30 p.m. when they would be supervised on retiring to bed.

'Doing the Bunk' or 'Midnight Walks', known as a feature of some boys' lives for many years, i.e., leaving the school grounds and returning undetected, was almost a sport for some, if we believe the boys' own words. A favourite 'escape' in the 1940s was to climb over the garden wall, buy fish and chips from David Davis' shop in North Street, and return for a dormitory feast. It must have been easy for people to recognise the Blue Coat Boys, and the shop owner or others may well have reported this escapade to the Headmaster, for on one occasion a second wave of boys was returning over the wall with their 'prize' to find Mr Spendlove, together with the first group, waiting for them. They were made to stamp on the fish and chips, and the following day they received 'six of the best'. There is also the poignant case of a boy escaping and going home, hiding in the garden, watching his mother make a drink and then returning to school, without his mother ever knowing of his visits. Less serious were the arranged meetings over the garden wall with relatives, often brothers or sisters, who would bring sweets, comics and even cigarettes—for some boys, a regular risk— and then there were those who met girl friends.

Over the years boys were made to perform other acts of mischief under peer pressure: younger boys had to climb on the roof of the covered way to fetch items thrown up there by older boys—or thrown in to the garden, which was also out of bounds. Boys, under threat, also had to trespass on neighbouring property before returning with evidence of a successful exploit. Invariably these bullying tactics were carried out just in time for the headmaster to appear.

Misdemeanours were not the prerogative of the boys alone. In 1868 the Trustees noted that there might be a risk that the Matron, Mrs Vick, was spoiling the boys 'by selling sweet-meats and articles' to them and that this was 'to be wholly discontinued'.

Of course, throughout the school's history there were expulsions for serious misbehaviour and it would not be fair to highlight them. Discipline at the school was always severe and it was not until the beginning of the 20th century that the severest punishments, such as flogging, withholding food and making boys perform unreasonable physical work, were discontinued. In 1893, however, a 'charge made of the Master for undue chastisement of the two boys ... was entered into'. (It appears the boys and parents did not appear, so the Trustees listened only to Mr Ballard). The account continues, 'After considering the case and inspecting the canes used, the Trustees concluded that the Master had not been guilty of undue severity'.

The alternative punishment to the excesses of former years, introduced in 1908 by Charles Fairbrother, required boys to write out from one hundred to a thousand words depending on the seriousness of the crime. They were also made to write out and learn poetry. The Headmaster, we understand, had a 'Black Book' in which the boys' misconduct would be noted and a points system was used to measure long-term behaviour. One boy in 1911 tells us that the severest punishment he suffered was 'having three and a half hours home time stopped'. (At this time local boys were allowed home on Saturday evenings. This practice was stopped in the 1920s to prevent truancy.) Although flogging had been abolished, we know that caning did not stop. During the last five years of the school a number of boys have painful memories of this punishment, which, after all, had been until very recently an accepted means of school discipline. Perhaps one of the most unusual forms of punishment, according to one boy, was 'cutting the grass on the cricket pitch with scissors', apparently for acknowledging his parents while marching within the City limits.

As may be expected, a number of boys speak of the discipline as being too severe and the restriction distressing, but many boys who, after school, joined the armed services, mainly the Royal Navy, considered that school life was a great experience and prepared them for the harsh life to come. They consider they had a head start on other recruits. The school moulded outstanding characteristics, cleanliness, honesty to one peers, good time-keeping and self discipline. The lifestyle brought all pupils together, teaching both tolerance and the ability to work together to achieve a common purpose.

Surprisingly, food, surely one of the more important factors, receives only scant references throughout the early years and in most cases not from the boys but rather from the Trustees. In 1720 expenditure for 'Brandy Lemons and sugar for punch' whilst viewing the timber at Wittering and again in 1775, 'Choice Lobsters' and many times 'refreshment at the farm' were all noted. However, the purchase in 1712 of a 'Powdered Tub to Salt a quarter of beefe' does reassure us that the boys were to be properly fed. For much of the 1700s and 1800s, most meat was salted, cooked and served cold with onions and basic vegetables such as cabbage and potatoes, which would be un-peeled. Recipes from the period are for 'ham pye', 'lamb pye' and of course pigeon pie; these may not have been part of the boys' regular diet, but we can be certain that the boys' food would have been rather plain, though there would be enough. During the 19th century occasionsally the Trustees felt it necessary to comment on the boys' meals. For example, in 1832 the Trustees tell us that after a Charity Sermon, in the Cathedral, the boys returned for 'Plum Duff and Beer'. In January 1839, the Trustees visited the school and 'saw the boys at dinner' when they had 'a cold beef, hot potatoes and good Beer'. On the occasion of the wedding of the Prince of Wales in 1863 the 'Blue Coat Boys had a glorious dinner of Roast Beef,

44 The Dining Hall, *c.*1920s. The boards on the left and right of the fireplace listed past and present Governors and Trustees. The four Flemish wooden panels over the fireplace are said to have been excavated from the site during the re-building of the school, 1904-6, although it is more likely that they were recovered from the original demolished school building. Two of the panels are now in the Chichester District Museum, while the other two are at Christ's Hospital.

Plum Pudding and Cake'. In 1879 Headmaster Ballard was authorised to 'purchase an eighteen gallon cask of beer for the boys, to be given to them at their dinner in about the proportion of a pint to four boys'.

We are fortunate to have a more detailed resumé of the boys' diet from the beginning of the 20th century. Charlie Howard, butcher, of North Street was supplying beef, pork, veal and mutton at this time. It was apparently of very good quality, if rather fat. But still the meat was served cold though well cooked. The boys only had hot meat in stews, usually beef and liver, once every two weeks. Pudding was always served first, a tradition in England from the 17th century, which ensured that boys would not be so hungry when the meat dish, which would be more expensive, was served. Mostly these were suet puddings, known to the boys as duff, cooked in a thick square slab, sliced horizontally with jam or treacle spread on the slices and then cut into square portions. Rice pudding was served twice a week and occasionally bread pudding, often at the end of term to use up the stale bread. The boys drank milk and water at breakfast and at midday, but tea with their evening meal.

From 1906, when the new building opened, meals were taken in the large dining room. The boys still used the four original refectory style tables, now at Christ's Hospital, with heavy wooden benches, each table seating 10 boys. They were arranged two on either side of the room with the Headmaster's table completing a 'U' shape. It was a rather grand room with oak panelling on all four walls. Although not austere, there was a severe and sobering atmosphere. The walls were festooned with deer antlers together with an enormous set of buffalo or bull horns, having a spread of some five or six feet. A large glass case had been installed, known by the boys as 'the museum'. It contained, among many items now lost to memory, an emu's egg and at least one cannonball, presumed to be from the siege of Chichester in 1642, and recovered when the old school building was demolished. There was another glass case containing a beautiful model sailing ship, *Jamnagar*, which had been presented to the school in 1945 by the shipbuilders Messrs Thornycroft Ltd.

From a number of pictures, the most important was the portrait of the founder, Oliver Whitby, painted in 1684, which for many years of its early life had been in the possession of Gilbert White of Selborne, who was a distant relative. The painting was acquired by a group of Old Oliver Whitbyians in 1887 and presented to the school. Also, in 1906, at the expressed wish of Old Boys, a 'screen' was erected in the dining room, behind the Headmaster's table, listing the names of all the Trustees from 1702. Grace was said before every meal and silence was demanded throughout mealtimes; any boy caught talking or seen using sign language was called out and made to stand in front facing the whole school and would forego his meal. In an attempt to overcome the shortage of food during the Second World War the Government required all who had a garden or an allotment to 'Dig for Victory'. The boys lived up to this by working in the Headmaster's garden, growing many of their vegetables. Also, to ensure no lack of nourishment in their diet, boys recall collecting stinging nettles from around the playing field. These were then washed, boiled and served with their rations of meat and potatoes. There are mixed views as to the flavour of this 'delicacy', but they do remember the painful experience of collecting them!

However, boys agree that most of the time they never went hungry. They could always fill up on 'tokes' served in very old wooden trays. (Boys always referred to bread as 'tokes'; the *Complete Oxford Dictionary* lists its meaning as 'pieces of bread' and quotes Charles Dickens as an early user of the word.)

Boys were allowed a boiled egg on their birthdays and this appears to have been the only time the boys had eggs. This is borne out by the story of a boy who, whilst at the playing field, discovered a pheasant's nest with an egg in it and, on mentioning it to Mr Spendlove, he was told to take it back for breakfast. The following morning Matron served him the egg, with envious gasps from other boys. He was probably, he claimed, the only boy to have two eggs in one year!

Although the food was monotonous—the same meals being served on the same days week after week—there were favourites: 'Sausage fat' (type of dripping) and 'Treacle Hardbake' (an over cooked suet pudding). Boys who scrubbed the wooden schoolroom floors at the end of term had a treat in the form of a pork pie. There is mention of strawberries being plentiful during the summer of 1931, a basket, two pounds in weight, costing three 'old pence'. A type of Yorkshire Pudding, known to the boys as 'panyan' and served as a pudding with jam, treacle or just sugar, proved such a favourite it was often used as an item for 'trading' with other boys for favours carried out or as a swop for treats from home.

The school never had a great many traditions, but boys recall the most important as Founder's Day, 19 February, when each year they would march to a ceremony held in front of the Founder's memorial within the Cathedral's south cloister. Many boys recall the annual visit of H. M. Inspector which meant examinations, bringing a welcome change to routine. Always popular was the tradition of prize-giving, at which boys were called upon to recite a piece of poetry they would have learned during the term. These would often be popular poems such as Gray's *Elegy* and G.K. Chesterton's *The Donkey*. At the end of Christmas term, during Mr Spendlove's Headship, boys would perform in a play for parents and guests, often with the Headmaster and Matron taking part. In July was the annual presentation of the House Shield, together with the Fairbrother Memorial Prize and the announcement of the Head Boy for the following year. Tradition was that the Head Boy's name would be added, in gold leaf, to the School's Roll of Honour Board (see Appendix III).

45   Members of the Old Oliver Whitbyians Association at the 16th annual reunion dinner, 3 October 1956.

On Saturday 30 October 1931, at the *Dolphin Hotel* in Chichester, 120 people sat down to dinner on the occasion of the first annual reunion of the Old Oliver Whitbyians Association. Sir William Bird J.P. was the first President and Mr F.W. Weaver, the first Chairman. Also in attendance was the newly appointed Headmaster, Mr H.A. Spendlove, together with two sons of the late Headmaster, Mr Charles Fairbrother. Both boys had attended the school at some time. In recognition of a suggestion for a prize to be awarded in the school, the Trustees generously placed a fund at the Association's disposal so that a prize to be known as the 'Fairbrother Prize' should be given annually to 'the most popular boy in the school'. This tradition continued until the school closed. Although it had taken 229 years for the Association to be formed, those present were enthusiastic that it should be successful and flourish. This it has done for 71 years, 53 of these after the closure of the school, and although regular meetings are not now always possible, a memorable tercentenary celebration for the Founder and his school was held in 2002. Just as at the inaugural dinner there was an octogenarian, Mr Pryer, who had been at the school between 1857-9, so at the dinner held in 2002 there was 82-year-old Mr Stewart Trodd, who attended the school from 1929 to 1934.

An Oliver Whitby, Blue Coat Boy, left the school with his head held high, and a tear in his eye as he went through the Tower Street door for the last time.

———•———

This Chapter cannot be concluded without listing all the Old Boys whose memories and reminiscences have provided an insight into the formal and informal life of the School. The author's grateful thanks, therefore, go to:

1887–1899

1887–1890	R.C. Joyce	1891–1893	W.M. Holder
1893–1897	H.W. Shalders	1894–1896	E.G. Downer
1896–1900	S. Bacon	1899–1902	H.I. Anscombe

1900–1916

1901–1903	J. Edam	1901–1904	C.F.P. Heath
1902–1905	H. Ide	1904–1909	E.G. Brewer
1909–1912	L.J.H. Strudwick	1910–1914	W.C. Marsh
1912–1916	J.J. Saxton	1914–1919	A.G. Bridle
1916–1920	F.H. Putman		

1920–1929

1920–1924	W.G. Challen	1920–1925	V.C. Eade
1920–1925	J. Hoskins	1923–1928	H.F. Cates
1925–1929	E.K. Chandler	1925–1930	L.F.S. Savage
1926–1929	R.P. Carver	1926–1930	A.E. Cozens
1926–1931	W.H.F. Stillwell	1929–1932	B.N. Ballantyne
1929–1934	F.F. Forder	1929–1932	A.L. Turner
1929–1933	P.D.G. May	1929–1934	S.A. Trodd

1930–1939

1931–1934	E.C. Stillwell	1931–1935	R.F.G. Jellett
1932–1936	S.J.E. Dearling	1933–1937	G. Shier
1934–1939	D. Dibley	1934–1936	K.H.R. Scott
1934–1939	A.T. Shippam	1934–1939	E.C. Weller
1936–1941	R.A. Burnand	1937–1942	D.C. Baker
1938–1940	P.J.P. Fletcher	1939–1943	E.C. Billinghurst

1940–1949

1941–1945	W.J. Barnes	1941–1946	A.G.B. Carter
1941–1945	D.E. Rogers	1942–1946	L.R. Burnand
1942–1947	R.J. Lawrence	1942–1947	G.R. West
1943–1948	M.G. Page	1945–1949	J. Haffenden
1945–1948	R.G. Ide	1945–1949	D. Johnson
1947–1949	D.P. Welch	1948–1949	A.M. Philmore

The author's grateful thanks also go to the following friends of Oliver Whitby School: W.J. Heath, M.Merritt, F.A. Stenning.

Seven

Epilogue: All Was Not Lost

The School closed at the end of the Christmas term 1949 but it was not until 17 October 1951 that the Scheme governing the old Oliver Whitby Foundation of 26 October 1904 was repealed and a new Scheme (No. 3536 P.) was made by the Minister of Education under the Charities Acts, 1853 to 1925 and named the Oliver Whitby Educational Foundation.

The objective of this new Scheme was to take over the physical and financial assets of the 1904 Scheme so as to be able to continue to foster the charitable and educational aims as set out in Oliver Whitby's 1702 will.

The old 1902 Scheme was beset with regulations governing the running of the School. As the School had now closed, it was necessary to recognise this and to make modifications to the Rules and Regulations governing the actions of the New Foundation Governors. These were only achieved after the Ministry eventually was able to broker compromises between on the one side the Old Governors, and on the other the Diocesan Education authorities, being essentially, in this instance, the Dean and Chapter. Both were, in effect, continuing the 1949 conflict between them, as is evidenced by their correspondence with, and visits to, the Ministry.

The Dean and Chapter, having become aware of the School's difficulties in mid-1949, were very concerned about the local impact of the likely closure of the School. One of its members, Archdeacon Lancelot Mason, had some very informal and personal communications with Walter Stride, a Foundation Governor and prominent in City affairs. He wished to sound out the possibilities of a merger with the Prebendal School. It was both sad and unfortunate that Walter Stride died on 16 December that year.

At the same time, Admiral Phipps Hornby was negotiating with Christ's Hospital with the aim that Christ's Hospital should, by the sponsorship of local boys, be the recipient of all available Oliver Whitby funds. It is significant that on 4 November Jack Symonds, the Clerk, wrote to F.R.S. Keys, Chairman of the Oliver Whitbyians Association, informing him of the impending closure of the School and of the possible scheme—to sponsor boys at Christ's Hospital.

On 15 November 1949, in answer to Jack Symonds' enquiries about the procedure to sponsor boys, R.C. Evans, Clerk to the Council of Almoners of Christ's Hospital, advised that it was first necessary for boys from the catchment/beneficial area to have reached a certain level of academic ability. He proposed that 'qualifying boys should first pass the Local Authorities Examination for entry into Secondary Schools—this saves both the time and expense of an independent examination. If your Governors wish to adopt such a plan, all they need to do is to advertise the vacancies in the beneficial area, put the candidate through the County exam and nominate (say) 3 candidates in order of merit for final selection by our Headmaster'. He then went on, 'The second point is less important; it is necessary to ask how many places you wish to fill each year and when you wish to start. I understand that you will eventually have about £2,500 p.a., so 1 thought that 1 ought to get authority for you to have up to (say) 12 places ...' On 8 December 1949, The Council of Almoners agreed with this proposal, subject to Ministry of Education approval of the Scheme.

On 14 December the Clerk wrote to R. C. Evans that a decision '... had been reached after exhaustive consideration of alternative proposals ...' and, as a result, the Governors were going ahead with the closure of the School and the preparation of a new Scheme to sponsor boys at Christ's Hospital. On 21 December Admiral Phipps Hornby, the Chairman, made a speech at the closing ceremony and this was reported in the local press.

At their next meeting on 14 February 1950 the Governors agreed that Horace Albert Spendlove be paid a pension. He had been Headmaster from 1931 until the School's closure. He became 60 on 25 June 1960.

At the same meeting the Governors agreed to put in hand the sale of the 'physical assets' of the Trust, the buildings, land, etc., and the preparation of a new Scheme for agreement with the Ministry of Education.

Within a few days (18 February 1950), Eric Banks, Chichester Town Clerk, wrote to say that '... the Corporation would wish to acquire ...' the Parkland's Playing Fields 'as it is completely surrounded by land which the Corporation have already agreed to purchase as a site for housing ...'. These were the School's playing fields and pavilion by Sherborne Road, Chichester marked by the obelisk recording the gift of the field to the School by Captain Weller-Poley in memory of his son killed in the Great War. The obelisk still remains and it is ironic that the fields have not been built on and are still today very much as they were in 1950.

But there was competition for the field. On 7 March A.G. Bridle, a partner in Whitehead and Whitehead, Chichester estate agents (he was later to become a New Foundation Governor), wrote to tell that the WSCC had offered £1,000 for the field and 'lit would seem that the Governors have little alternative but to await a settlement of differences between the two authorities, as acceptance of this [WSCC] offer may well result in a very embarrassing position, particular if the City Corporation serve notice to compulsory purchase. The attitude of the District Valuer in such a position is an unknown quantity ...' In the event the District Valuer placed a value of £1,100 on the site and it was agreed to sell to the Corporation at this price plus 31 weeks rent at £1 per week occupation prior to the sale.

The main physical assets were the freehold buildings in the city. These consisted of the fine Schoolhouse in West Street with its garden and Gymnasium opening onto Chapel Street, and the cottage 52 Tower Street that was sold on 27 August 1951.

The Chichester property agents Whitehead & Whitehead and Jackson Stops & Staff were asked to advise whether to sell the freehold school buildings, alternatively, grant a lease thereon for 21 years, or grant a 99-year Ground Lease for either £10,000/5,000.

Whiteheads advised the Governors to sell with a reserve price of £22,500, which the Governors increased to £25,000. In due course the agents advertised the buildings, prior to the sale by auction on 28 June 1950, as being 'Ripe for development as Shops and Offices'. But the situation was not quite so simple.

The buildings were sold, in the first instance, to a Mr K.C. Rees-Reynolds for a net total of £29,199. His idea was to sell on the School House and cottage for £20,500 to Morants Ltd (the department store which was subsequently a branch of the Army & Navy and then the House of Fraser). However, the proceeds were not paid over until the 'planning' position had been clarified. The Post Office informally had agreed to buy the remaining buildings. They had wanted the Gymnasium for some time to replace it with a modern Telephone Exchange behind its main Post Office. This sale too was held up for clearance of the planning position; i.e. for the proposed use of the School building as a shop.

On 29 September 1950, a City Architect Brian Tyler wrote refusing planning consent on the grounds that '... such development would interfere with the amenities of the city ...'.

On enquiry, Eric Banks, Town Clerk, on behalf of the Corporation, wrote on 20 November—some three months after the sale—raising the following objections to the change of use:

a)   the School building was opposite the Cathedral and amongst fifteenth-century buildings;
b)   any change would spoil the special character of this western approach to the city with its many buildings of historic importance;
c)   the Corporation were opposed to any further commercialisation of the area;
d)   the introduction of more shops should be prevented ...

Suffice it to say, on 23 November 1950 the planning refusal was withdrawn and the monies could be paid over but it was not until 11 June 1951 that contracts were finally signed and payments made.

For achieving this and the successful auction, etc., Whiteheads were paid £1,010 0s. 9d.

In total, together with the monies from sale of the playing field and 52 Tower Street, a total of £32,005.75 was raised. This total also included the proceeds from the sale of Furniture (£1,010); Household linen (£39); Coal (£22); Clothing (£56.75); Stationery (£57); Provisions (£6); and other items (£515).

The documentation of the new Scheme required the listing of the assets inherited by the new Governors. By October 1951 the net cash proceeds of the sale, after the continuing and closing expenses and income of the Trust, amounted to £32,053 7s. 10d. cash at Barclays Bank. On 15 December 1951 the Clerk informed the Ministry that he had invested £31,000 of this by the purchase of £10,500 each of 4% Consols, 3% Savings Bonds 65/75, and 3½% Conversion Stock.

In addition to the 'physical' assets sold there were also two other 'Properties' listed in the Schedule of Property attached to the formal new Scheme document. These were:

a) Common Farm, West Wittering; and
b) School, Schoolmaster's House, and buildings, West Wittering.

Both of these were listed at nil value. This was just as well as both were eventually considered by the Governors of the time to be worthless ... 8 December 1951, the County Librarian, B. Campbell Cook, wrote to the Clerk saying that he was '... concerned about preservation of records ... particularly the map of Property in West Wittering, but I presume there are probably title deeds ...' How right his concern proved to be.

The Common Farm (sometimes referred to as the Charity Farm) consisted of approximately 2½ acres of land with a thatched barn and hovel, to the north of Piggery Hall Lane at Itchenor

Cross Roads, West Wittering, let at £30, plus five quarters of wheat, p.a. to the Personal Representatives of Mrs Florence Fanny Shrubb. For some reason, it had been 'demised and granted' by the Prebend of West Wittering prior to 1900. It was listed as 'Property' in the Schedule attached to the 1902 Scheme, being an 'Indenture Lease' to the Trust for so long as any one of three of children of HRH Duke of Connaught (son of Queen Victoria) was still alive, under the doctrine of 'cestui que vires'. These were HRH Princess Margaret of Connaught (who became Queen of Sweden and who died on 1 May 1920), HH Prince Alexander Albert of Battenberg (Marquis of Carisbrooke who died during 1960), HH Princess Patricia of Connaught (Lady Patricia Ramsay who died on 14 January 1974). It was the custom in Victorian times, and just afterwards, to determine a specific date in a legal document (e.g. the ending of a lease, the passing of gifted monies, etc.) by associating this with the happening of an ensured event—and nothing is so sure as death. The date of death of these three Royals is also relevant to three insurance policies held by the Governors.

On 15 July 1920, following the death of the Swedish princess, it was thought necessary to draw up a new, seven-page indenture between the Rev. Robert Henry Codrington, vicar of West Wittering, and the then Governors.

On 15 January 1952 the Clerk wrote to Strides, Surveyors, Auctioneers, Valuers and Estate Agents to enquire into the possibilities of obtaining vacant possession, with an indication of what the probable value to the Governors would be, or alternatively, the option of increasing the rent.

Strides' advice on 19 January to the Governors was:

– As the Barn was about to collapse, to get release from the lease as soon as possible with no dilapidation being payable
– as the ground was too wet for the growing of corn, no increase in rent could be entertained.

Accordingly, Jack Symonds wrote to John Widdows, of T. Macdonald Eggar, J.S. Widdows, Solicitors, in his capacity of Clerk to the Dean and Chapter, to say that '... the Governors' were prepared to sell back the lease for £120 with a release of any claim for dilapidations, and costs of sale'. On 6 June 1952 and after calling for a copy of the surveyors report, unsurprisingly but politely, this offer was turned down. It is not known when the lease was ended but the sum of £208 'Dilapidations' was paid during 1964. In any event, all would have been over on the death of Lady Ramsay in 1974.

The Schoolmaster's house, in the grounds of the West Wittering C.of E. Primary School in Pound Road, was listed on the Schedules to both the 1902 and the new Schemes, as being rented out at 2s. 6d. p.a., to the Education Department of the West Sussex County Council. However, from day one of the new Foundation—and before—WSCC Educational Department had actually paid £1 p.a. for the occupation house. In early 1975, Arthur Floyd, Foundation Governor and, as The County Chief Engineer, previously the WSCC representative Governor, realised that the house was no longer being occupied by any of the school's staff. It was learned, from the WSCC, that it was being rented to Mrs E.M. Holroyd, Headmistress of Chichester Rumboldswhyke C.of E. School on a monthly tenancy, at £204 p.a.—a far cry from the £1 p.a. being paid to the Foundation ...

On 22 January 1975, Robert Burdett, by now the Clerk, suggested to the Governors that, as one of the Trust's objects is the provision of education for boys in West Wittering, the Foundation might well be happy to continue with the peppercorn rent. However, the Governors decided that they had an over-riding duty to obtain a market rent for the schoolhouse. In a letter to the WSCC, they suggested that, at the next WSCC meeting on 4 March, the Director of Education be given certain discretionary limits to negotiate a more realistic rent at the meeting to be held with Peter Hanbury and Arthur Floyd on 18 April.

In the meantime, Arthur Floyd discovered that this inequitable situation had existed for some time. Mr Harris, when he was Headmaster and had occupied the house, had also being paying £204 p.a. The Clerk was asked to get in touch with Glenister Woodger, the West Wittering estate agent, to obtain advice. A compromise was made and on 5 September, E.M. Holdsworth, County Secretary, wrote to confirm the terms agreed on 18 April for a new full repairing lease of the schoolhouse at £150 p.a. for five years.

Around that time, the WSCC were faced with the need to expand the West Wittering primary school. Two main options were under consideration. The first was to move the school to a new site in nearby Summerfield Road. The second was to remodel the present buildings in Pound Road. On 24 September, Mr Holdsworth wrote to the Clerk that WSCC were '... considering a feasibility study to ascertain whether the premises can be structurally improved and remodelled at reasonable cost'. Should this be undertaken, then, the WSCC needed security of tenure. He had looked through the Deeds in the County Council's possession, back to the start of the Education Act in 1944, ant could find no reference to the Foundation's ownership of the school or any covenants that might affect the WSCC position. He asked the Clerk for an 'Abstract of titled' or any other information available.

Despite an extensive search, the Clerk was unable to unearth any substantiation of the Foundation's legal right of ownership. Thus this source of income dried up ...

Part I of the Schedule of Property, eventually attached to the documentation of the new 1951 Scheme, showed that as well as the £32,005.75 monies raised by the sale of the physical assets, the 'new' Governors inherited a total (at cost price) of £69,456 investments producing £1,976 income p.a. These investments were:

- £55,440.75 Government Stocks and Savings Bonds invested with the Official Trustees of Charitable Funds (yielding £1,571.45 p.a.)
- £14,013.45 with the Governors of Queen Anne's Bounty (yielding £404.73 p.a.).

Investing in such stocks had first started as long ago as 1767 with the purchase of £200 Capital Stock in 4% Consols.

An additional investment listed was the 'P.W. Jamieson Fund'. Jamieson had been an Old Oliver Whitbyian. In his will he left the life interest in 5,000 Canadian Pacific Railway Common Shares to his widow, who died in September 1945. On her death, the shares came to the Governors and were sold for £879, and were invested in £882 15s. 7d. 2½% Consols. The £22 1s. 4d. p.a. income arising therefrom was then used to provide outings for pupils at the School.

On Part II of the Schedule are listed two Policies of Insurance. The first, for £1,000 plus profits was with Sun Life (premium £18 p.a.), the proceeds becoming payable on the death of the Marquis of Carisbrooke. He died during 1960 and £1,845 was received.

The second for £3,000 plus profits was with Phoenix Assurance (premium £52 p.a.) the proceeds becoming payable on the death of Lady Patricia Ramsay. She died on 14 January 1974. Phoenix 'in the particular circumstances of the case' (sic) wrote that they were prepared to accept an extract of her *The Times* obituary as evidence of her death. By that time, the £3,000 had become, with annual bonuses, £17,493.80. After some haggling, an additional *ex gratia* payment of £82.37 for interest on late payment was received. It is interesting to note that, in May that year, Barclays Bank Treasury Dept interest rate for deposits of five months was 13.5% ...

Thus, on the formation of the new Scheme in October 1951, the total of the listed investments was shown as £69,454 (yielding £1,976.18 p.a.), plus the £32,053.35 balance of the monies from the sales of the school buildings etc., giving a grand total of £101,507.35.

The listed £1,976 annual income became approximately £1,700, after the annual payment of the two Insurance Premiums of £70 p.a., £32 p.a. to Thomas Eggar for 'Corn rent' on the 'Common land', and the pension to the last Headmaster, Mr Horace A. Spendlove until his death on 26 November 1974.

As Christ's Hospital fees in the early 1950s were around £228 p.a., the Governors were confident that they would be able to carry on the charitable spirit of Oliver Whitby's will (subject to the rules and regulations of the new Scheme eventually being agreed with the Ministry of Education).

The new Scheme could not be finalised until the old Trust properties had been sold and a final statement of affairs prepared. Throughout 1950 and 1951, whilst this was going on and the deals were being struck, the Governors were actively seeking to have the Rules & Regulations of a new Scheme drawn up and approved by the Ministry of Education. However, the old 1949 antagonism between the Church and the Governors was still apparent. On 7 December 1950 the Governors' first draft of the Regulations for a new Scheme, based on the old 1902 Scheme, was sent to the Ministry. There was then a meeting at the Ministry between Mr Henty, the Clerk, and G.R. Hughes the Ministry's case officer. From then on Mr Hughes took a keen interest, as will be seen.

In view of the strong Church of England emphasis in Oliver Whitby's will, Bishop Bell went to the Ministry again, this time with Archdeacon Lancelot Mason, and the Rev. Guy Middleton (Diocesan Educational Department). In addition to wishing to have a Diocesan representative on the new Board, the Ministry of Education also were insisting that the Bishop of Chichester, from time to time, be on the governing body of the new Foundation. After this meeting, G.R. Hughes wrote to the Bishop saying, '... I am not at all unhopeful of a satisfactory outcome ...'.

However, the Old Governors too were still fighting a rearguard action. They wrote to the Ministry saying

> ... one representative of the Chichester Diocesan Committee is sufficient in as much as the Committee has in the past no official representation on the Board of Governors and the local authorities have only one representative each. Whilst the Governors held the Bishop in the highest esteem [they were] of the opinion that the appointment of the Bishop as an *ex officio* Governor is an innovation which [they felt] unable to accept in principle. This suggestion is not made on any personal grounds, but as already stated, as a matter of principle.

G.R. Hughes proposed a compromise and the Governors had to accept this. Perhaps it was this capitulation by the Governors that prompted the Bishop to agree on 26 July to the compromise whereby he and his successors should not be governors of the new Scheme but that the number of 'representative' Governors be increased to three by the addition of a representative of the Chichester Diocesan Educational Department.

The Governors were not inactive in scrutinising every word of the new Scheme. The following gives three illustration of this. The Ministry's amended draft regulation governing 'Application of Income', stated that the Governors shall apply their net income to assist in the education of boys '... at Christ's Hospital or any other school...'. The Governors wished that the word 'primarily' be inserted before 'at Christ's Hospital'. On 23 June 1950 the Ministry wrote to the Governors saying

> ... as the Diocese ... were anxious for the income or part of it to be devoted to the Prebendal School and the line we have taken all through is that we should not tie the present and future Governors to spending their money on any particular schools, but that we must leave the expenditure to their discretion and wisdom in the light of current conditions, giving them as wide a power as possible. We have gone as far as we can to meet you ... by mentioning Christ's Hospital by name.

The Ministry had in mind the representations of Bishop Bell and the doctrine of 'cy pres' (that a gift be made as near as possible to the testator's or donor's intentions when these cannot be precisely followed). Despite another visit to the Ministry by Mr Henty and the Clerk on 6 July, it was only right and equitable that the Ministry should prevail and the Governors had to accept that 'primarily' should be omitted. The Governors had to accept this.

The Ministry's final wording of the Application of Income Rule 12 reads:

> (1) After payment of any expenses of administration, the Governors shall apply the income of the Foundation in granting scholarships or awards for the benefit of qualified boys, to assist in their education or training at Christ's Hospital, or any other school where religious instruction is given according to the doctrines of the Church of England, or at any university or other place of learning, or to enable them to prepare for, or assist their entry into, some profession, trade or calling, and for that purpose may provide them with outfits, clothing, tools, instruments, or books.

The Governors' leaning towards sponsorship at Christ's Hospital was thus preserved but their permitted use of available funds had been considerably broadened.

Both Harting and West Wittering folk were concerned about the proposed extension of the 'qualifying residential area'. On 19 December 1950, Morris, wrote on behalf of the Managers of Bew, & Bailey, Solicitors of 4 West Pallant, West Wittering School (the Rev. Lawrence Blackall then the Vicar of West Wittering) objecting to the enlargement of the 'catchment area' by the inclusion of the rural districts of Chichester and Midhurst. On 4 January 1951, G.R. Hughes replied pointing out that both West Wittering and Harting were '... especially privileged areas ... and it is the Minister's duty to apply the *cy pres* doctrine when making a new scheme. To satisfy any proposal restricting the benefits might even cause a fresh failure of the trust'.

In Clause 2 of the Application of Income Rule, the Minister, clarified the position, and ruled:

> (2) In this clause the expression 'qualified boys' means boys whose parents are members of the Church of England, are in need of financial assistance and who are and have been for not less than two years *bona fide* residents in the City of Chichester or in the Rural Districts of Chichester or Midhurst: provided that a preference shall be given to boys resident in the City of Chichester or in the Parishes of Harting or West Wittering and as nearly as may be in each year in the following proportions, should fit candidates present themselves, that is to say, three-fifths from the city of Chichester, and one-fifth each from the Parishes of Harting and West Wittering. If, in any year, a sufficient number of fit candidates from Chichester, Harting and West Wittering respectively do not present themselves, the Governors may, subject to the preference aforesaid, fill up the number from qualified boys from any of the other places.

On 15 March 1951, in answer to the Governors' request to the Ministry for a definition of 'member of the Church of England', G. R. Hughes wrote that the Ministry's legal advisor, after writing to the Bishop of St Edmundsbury and Ipswich, advised that

> ... his conclusion was that there was no procedure laid down by law as generally applicable for deciding who was such a member and that any decision must depend on factors giving rise to the query. I see that there is an interesting case of Perry Almshouses 1898. ... The view of the Dean Church [sic] is that a solemn declaration made by the individual concerned is sufficient. This may be poor law, but it is not a bad practice ....

The Ministry's amended draft had used the term 'Co-optative' Governors (elected by the votes of the members). They wished to continue the term 'Foundation' and the Ministry accepted this.

During these protracted negotiations, the Clerk was in correspondence with R.C. Evans, the Clerk to Christ's Hospital, to clarify the procedure for the selection and sponsorship of boys at Horsham. It had been planned that the formation of the new Foundation be announced during Christ's Hospital 1951 Speech Day. In view of the delay, on 11 June Mr Evans informed the Headmaster that he had '... better not make any reference to the Scheme on Speech Day in the Senior Grecian's speech ...'.

The delay in the completion of the Scheme prevented any possibility of sponsoring full-time education for boys at Christ's Hospital, or anywhere else, during 1951. The first recorded 'sponsorship' was payments in June 1952 of bus fares for Old Whitbyians, still of school age, to travel to Midhurst Grammar School and the Lancastrian—Richard Doncaster £10, Arthur David Spencer £14 12s. 6d. and Ivan Courtney £13 8s. 6d. who had a further 8 guineas in April 1953 to travel up from Wittering to the Lancastrian.

It was not until 8 December 1952 that an invitation for applicants for grants was placed in both the *Chichester Observer* and *West Sussex Gazette*. (In later years advertising was extended to the Petersfield press.) This resulted in a flood of requests for the form—the start of the formal processing of candidates—confirming eligibility of age, residence, membership of Church of England, parental income, etc. The honour of being the very first applicant (17 December) belongs to Mrs D.H. Beveridge, West Wittering, for her son David Anthony. (Unfortunately David was not accepted, being too young to qualify.)

Altogether there were 16 requests for the form—Harting (2), West Wittering (4), Chichester (8), Birdham (1), and a very late request from as far as Horsham ...

On 26 February Christ's Hospital wrote to the Clerk with their then scales of parental income above which no grant would be considered. These were: Parent(s) with one dependant child £675; two £775; three £875; four £975; and £100 for each additional child.

Many of the candidates were found not to meet the eligibility rules. Those who did were asked to take the County exam. In the end three boys were selected for interview. This must have been a daunting affair for the young candidates. On 23 June 1953, H.L.O. Flecker, O.B.E., Christ's Hospital Headmaster, came down by train and was met and given luncheon at the *Dolphin*. He then gave the candidates an intelligence test. The boys were then interviewed by him and the Governors in the Magistrates Room, at the City Council Chambers in North Street.

Two boys were chosen to start in September 1953—John Archer (South Harting) and Christopher John Baker (Chichester). It is of note that both were sons of schoolteachers ... Christ's Hospital fees were then £226 p.a. and parental contributions Were £33 and £36 p.a. respectively. The Governors also supported Arthur Gilbert at £25 for two terms at Midhurst Grammar School. At last the new Foundation had started its work.

Sir William Barrott Montfort Bird, now 95 years old, but still nominally the Chairman, having been a Governor since 30 March 1916, retired, but the following five of the 'old guard' of governors were reappointed and became Foundation Governors within the new scheme

Admiral R.S. Phipps Hornby, C.M.G., of Lavington Manor. He became Chairman and was appointed for five years. He resigned on 17 February 1956. In August 1975, the Governors were informed by NatWest Bank that, by the generous terms of the Admiral's will, the Foundation was to be the beneficiary of a 'fund' payable on the death of the last survivor of his daughter Rosemary Ruth (who died on 9 December 1981), and her son Jeremy Rowley Spied Soote, his grandson. In June 1975, the then value of this fund, which arose from the sale of the Admiral's 317-acre Sindles Farm at Westbourne, was £13,800. The most recent value has been given as £65,274 (22 March 2002).

Arthur G. Bridle (an Old Oliver Whitbyian) who had handled Whiteheads Auction sale of the School buildings in 1951 succeeded Admiral Phipps Hornby on 9 December 1956. The minutes of the February 1975 Governors' meeting record that he reported that the Old Oliver Whitbyians Association had been revived and that he had been invited to and had attended their annual dance and had spoken on the work of the Foundation. The Clerk said that he was waiting for a list of old boys and hoped to trace them so that they could be put in touch with the Association. Although not greatly successful, due primarily to the fact that many of the Old Boys were in the services or had moved away, there were a number of meetings of Old Boys. However, the Association, which has now been disbanded, assisted in no small way in the success of the Tercentenary Celebrations in February 2002.

Engineer Admiral Sir R.W. Skelton, K.C.B., C.B.E., D.S.O., of Eartham, was appointed for four years. He also resigned on 17 February 1956. On 30 May 1950 he arranged that the model steamer, built by Thorneycroft and presented by them to the School in 1945, be sent to Christ's Hospital for display in their Manual Training School. Sets of coats and breeches, the oil painting of Oliver Whitby, and the old refectory tables also went to Christ's Hospital. On 28 March 1952 it was agreed with Eric Banks that the Corporation should have the statue of the blue boy (this stood on the great oak staircase of the School for many years but is now also at Christ's Hospital), a set of mounted coins, and the Flemish Oak carving, '... two double oak window shutters taken reportedly from Rookwood house, a property once owned by the Foundation ...'. It is now known that Rookwood House was once the home of Florence Fanny Shrubb. H.J. Ling succeeded the Admiral on 16 March 1956.

Brigadier O.L. Prior-Palmer, D.S.O., for four years, resigning 17 October 1963. During the 1940s he was MP for Worthing.

Richard Iltead Henty Esq., Chairman of Henty's Brewery in Westgate who lived in Oaklands House, Chichester, was appointed for three years. He served until his death on 18 February 1954. On 24 April he was succeeded by *John S. Widdows*, M.B.E., who was living in Wittering, senior partner of Thomas Eggar & Son, and Clerk to the Dean and Chapter (who had turned down the Governors' offer to sell the 'Common Land').

Admiral The Hon. Sir H. Meade-Fetherstonhaugh, G.C.V.O., C.B., D.S.O., of Uppark, was appointed for two years, having previously been the representative of the WSCC, resigning on 9 November 1962. On 5 July 1963, he was succeeded by *Peter F. Hanbury*, Hop Merchant and Landowner in South Harting, who in turn has been succeeded by his son Nigel, a member of the Council of Lloyds.

Arthur Floyd, County Chief Engineer and organist at West Wittering Church, was appointed a Foundation Governor (having been the representative of WSCC) on 7 February 1975. *Jack Symonds*, the Clerk, was also appointed a Foundation Governor that day until his death in August 1976. He reported that he had attended the funeral of Horace Spendlove who died on 26 November 1974. John *McKerchar, F.C.A.*, Wittering, ex-Chairman of Wingard (which had its automotive product factories in Chichester), was appointed in February 1977 and, on the retirement of Peter Hanbury in 2000, is the present Chairman. *R.H. Knight*, Chairman of Rowes Garage in Chichester, was appointed on 3 May 1979, retiring in 2000.

The other present Foundation members of the Board are *Clifford Spawton* who originally joined as City Council representative on 20 October 1983; *Capt. Taff Davies*, and *Mrs Sara Hammett JP*, Chairman of the Juvenile Bench of Chichester and Worthing, daughter of the well known Dr Wilfred Coultard of Chichester.

Following the heated exchanges in the closing days of the School, the number of 'Representative Governors' had been increased to three. The first such governors were: *Chichester Diocesan Education Committee*—This was the newly created additional appointment— The Venerable Lancelot Mason, Archdeacon of Chichester Cathedral. He had been a party to the 1949 negotiations about the merger of the School with the Prebendal that, sadly, came to nought—but more of this later. It had been the general practice over the years that the Archdeacon of Chichester should be the representative. Following the tragic death in 2001 of Archdeacon Keith Hobbs (whose wife Mary was the writer of the definitive historical survey of Chichester Cathedral), the position is presently held by the Rev. Robert D. Harris, Rural Dean of Arundel and Bognor.

West Sussex County Council—C. D. Herniman. On 17 October 1952 E.T. Evans succeeded him. Arthur Floyd followed, until his appointment as a Foundation Governor. It has been the practice since then for the representative to be a member of the WSCC Education Committee, although currently they are not represented.

Chichester City Council—G.A. Russell Purchase (wine merchant of North Street), resigned 17 October 1963 to be followed over the years by many eminent City Councillors. Presently the appointee is the Rev. John Rankin.

For many years, Raper & Co., Solicitors, 55/56 West Street, have provided the Clerk, first to the School and then to the new Foundation. At the time of the School's closure, Jack W. Symonds, Rapers' Accountant, was Clerk and he continued as Clerk to the new Foundation until he was appointed a Foundation Governor, continuing until his death in August 1976. Miss Valerie Bird, of Rapers, then took over and was followed by Michael G. Bevis, a partner in the firm until, in December 1973, he moved to join Rowntree & Bevis in Midhurst.

Lt Cmdr Robert P. Burdett then took over as Clerk. Having retired from the Royal Navy, he became articled to Rapers. Having qualified he left to join Burdett & Dyer, Solicitors in Havant in February 1974. 'I must say that we shall all miss your friendly face in the city' in the hand-over letter from Barclay's Bank, is an illustration of the high esteem in which he was held during his tenure of office.

On 1 March 1975, he handed over to the present Clerk, David John MacCahearty, a partner of Rapers.

By the School year 1958/59 Christ's Hospital's annual fees had risen from £226 p.a. to £280 p.a. The number of boys sponsored had also risen from two to eleven. After parental contributions, the annual costs to the Foundation had risen from £407 to £2,411.

It soon became apparent to Peter Hanbury, when he succeeded Admiral Meade-Fetherstonehaugh in 1963, that, unless income could be increased, sponsorship would have to be reduced. He set about reinvesting the Foundation's undated Consols in higher yielding dated COIF Funds and equities. These tactics proved to be a great success but the Foundation was by no means wealthy. Matters changed when, in 1979, the Governors inherited £88,854 from the estate of the late Roger Guy Halsted. He was a public benefactor and member of a well-known local family, one branch of which was the ironmonger in East Street, whose shop (according to T.G. Willis *Records of Chichester*) was blown up in the Autumn of 1871 by '… a 50 yr old trustworthy assistant drawing ½ pint of petroleum by candle light'.

By his will, Mr Halsted gifted his extensive land in the Westerton and Strettington areas to his wife, Edith Emily, to enjoy during her lifetime. On her death the proceeds were to be split into 24 equal parts. The first 12 parts were to named charities including Dr Barnardo's, St Dunstan's, British Legion, RNIB, British Red Cross, etc. The remaining 12 were to be selected by his wife with instructions that they be Charities for such organisations as dealt with orphans, the blind, folk disabled by war, etc., provided that they were not in receipt of Government funds. Mrs Halsted died in 1978. On the papers held at the offices of Wannop & Falconer (now Wannop & Fox), is noted the name of Oliver Whitby. During 1979 the Governors received the magnificent sum of £86,188.

By this time Peter Hanbury was Chairman. He, with Captain Robert (Bob) H. Knight, C.B.E., invested the Halsted bequest 50:50 in four dated Government stocks and in an equal spread of blue chip trading stocks. This had the effect of boosting the available income by £7,161 p.a. Shortly afterwards Anthony Dawson-Paul was appointed the Foundation's stockbroker. With his shrewd advice, the Governors succeeded in gradually building up the Foundation's capital so that, by the end of 1984, its total financial worth amounted to £484,000. 16 years later, on the Tercentenary of Oliver Whitby's death, this has increased by 285 per cent to over £1.3 million, with annual income over £52,000. But the cost of sponsorship has also increased. For example Christ's Hospital's annual fees in 2002 are £14,715. A far cry from the 1952/3 starting point of £226.

Since the start of the new Foundation in 1951, 35 boys have been at Christ's Hospital and two boys at Prebendal. From 1985 to August 2001, grants have totalled over £700,000 after parental contributions—£672,100 for scholars at Christ's Hospital and £45,500 at the Prebendal School. Grants in the year to August 2002 will cost £36,205. At today's costs grants will rise to £44,648 in 2003 for the four scholars sponsored at Christ's Hospital.

The Governors not only look after the funds, they also take a keen interest in the progress of the boys they sponsor. They receive regular school reports and, working closely with the schools' authorities, they are not slow to make their views known to any boy who is not taking proper advantage of the wonderful opportunity the Foundation provides.

Since the start, in October 1951, of the new Oliver Whitby Educational Foundation, Christ's Hospital in Horsham has become co-educational. Over the years at least two attempts have been made to persuade the Ministry of Education to extend the Governors' scope of sponsorship to include girls. But, as Oliver Whitby's will was specific on this point, no change has been permitted.

The Foundation is now well established and old enmities are long since buried. At the time of the closure of the School, there was a possibility of some scheme of integration with the Prebendal School. That was not to be. However, all stories should have a happy ending and this one is no exception.

The Prebendal School is in need of extra space and over many years the Oliver Whitby Governors held their meetings in the library of Rapers, 55/56 West Street. It is therefore significant that, in this Tercentenary year, the Foundation has agreed to loan £150,000 to the Prebendal School to help the school to buy the Rapers' building. A fitting start to the next 300 years.

Postscript

In December 1949, 48 boys walked out of the Tower Street school doors for the last time. Being launched into an unknown and cruel world, many left with similar fears and expectations to those first 12 boys who had come together 237 years before them. Depending on their ages, the leaving boys dispersed among a number of different schools to finish their education, or they proceeded to seek their fortune by finding employment. A few exchanged their regimented lives for another, by straightaway joining one of the armed services. Oliver Whitby's School had closed.

The building remained, and to this day is an important part of West Street's prospect of spire, tower and classic line, reflecting the attractive timeless architecture of Sir Reginald Blomfield. Almost a year after closing, on Thursday 7 September 1950, a sale was held to dispose of the school's effects. It is probably just as well that we are not able to know where all the furniture and objects, that meant so much to the boys' everyday lives, ended up. But, perhaps there is poignancy in that bread was the staff of life to every boy over all those years: 'Lot 289, Two [wooden] Bread Platters, Pastry Board and Lath Stand' was purchased by a Mrs Heath; the Bread Platters are now the proud possession of her son, Mr Wilfred Heath of Yapton in West Sussex. It is likely that the platters, each made from a single piece of wood, were used daily in the school for well over one hundred years.

After the sale of effects the building, for some time, was used by County Hall for storage. The neighbouring building of Morant's Department Store, which relocated to this site after their original premises were destroyed by enemy action during the Second World War, was taken over by the larger Army and Navy Stores group in 1955, and the management, on seeing the attraction of an extra several thousand square feet of selling space next door, entered into lengthy negotiations to buy the school building. This they finally did, and the new extension opened in 1964.

According to the eye-witness account of a store manager who entered the Old School on the day in the early 1960s when the keys were handed over:

> It was like entering a past era, secured in a time capsule. We felt that we were walking onto a film set. It was cold, and there was a stark sense of austerity throughout the building. The walls were painted a 'dirty' yellow with the lower half bottle-green, and to further this institutionalisation, a single flex with bare light bulb hung from the ceilings. Perhaps the most sobering sight was the Sick Room, short iron bedsteads, almost too small even for a child, with wafer thin horsehair mattresses. Windows so high it was impossible to see out. No evidence of home comforts, even when ill.
>
> Stark faded notices telling you where you were, Sickroom, Matron, Headmaster, others with stern instructions leaving no doubt as to what was expected of you, with signatures of names that must once have been held both in awe, and fear. All the wooden floors were either still highly polished, or scrubbed almost white.
>
> One grandiose sight within all the Spartanism was the large regal carved oak staircase, still glistening with polish applied over some forty years, day after day, by so many small hands. It would be almost

another forty years before anyone dared to alter this staircase and even then only by the minimum necessary to incorporate it into a modern department store.

Over the years, since the school closed, many Old Boys, or their sons, daughters and grandchildren wanting to bring alive the stories they had been told, have visited the Department Store asking to see the Old School. They would be taken to see areas which have now become offices and fashion departments. But with the front entrance, oval windows, oak staircase and part of the playgound still being there, it is often an emotional experience for many of them.

What became of the boys who attended this school? Unfortunately there are no such records. There were those who became successful artisans, tradesmen and public figures within their own City of Chichester. There were professionals: teachers, accountants, doctors, ministers of the church, writers and we know of at least one poet, William Collins, 1741. There were those who achieved success within the armed services, who fought and gave their lives in many cruel wars, but also those who survived—such as Douglas Groome, 1933, who in the R.A.F. flew 40 missions as a bomber pilot in the Second World War. And others for whom success lay in foreign lands, such as George Dawes, on whose behalf the Principals of two schools in South Africa with which he had been associated, on learning of the closure of the school, were prompted to write to the Governors regretting the closure and commenting on the contribution George had made to their schools. Indeed, the new hall of one of the schools is named after him, 'George Dawes Hall'.

Old Boys agree that the school was cold, basic and institutionalised. However, they never went without food and were well looked after. The education was superb, for the day, and they feel proud and very privileged to have been scholars at Oliver Whitby's School.

Appendix I

Trustees and Governors

1702-1718	George Gounter
1702-1722	Thomas Carr
1702-1710	Thomas Holt
1702-1735	Francis Goater
1702-1734	John Wakeford
1710-1730	Thomas Smith
1718-1730	Henry May
1722-1738	John Watts
1730-1744	John Costello
1730-1741	George Harris
1734-1738	Francis Allen
1738-1760	Sir Hutchins Williams, Bart.
1738-1764	Henry Peckham
1741-1777	Thomas Ludgate
1744-1760	George Stepney M.D.
1752-1754	John Parke
1753-1752	Richard Taunton
1754-1773	Sir John Miller, Bart.
1760-1784	William Milton
1760-1792	Richard Newland
1764-1777	Thomas Steale
1773-1777	Robert Bull
1777-1791	John Woods
1777-1792	Peckham Williams
1777-1817	James Piggott
1784-1831	John Peachey

1791-1834	John Woods
1792-1817	Francis Diggens
1792-1821	William Brereton
1817-1821	Sir George Murray K.C.B.
1817-1823	William Johnson
1821-1827	Sir James Brisbane K.C.B.
1821-1839	Charles Baker
1823-1846	George Farhill
1827-1866	Richard Hasler
1831-1837	Richard Buckner
1834-1869	William L. Woods
1837-1867	Edward W. Pilkington
1839-1869	William Newland
1846-1872	Francis Smith
1866-1896	John Baxton
1867-1890	John J. Johnson Q.C.
1869-1901	William W. Hasler
1869-1916	John W. Woods
1872-1898	Nicholas Tyacke M.D.
1890-1901	Sir Archibald Levin Smith M.R.P.C.
1896-1924	Thomas Weller-Poley
1898-1904	George Ashley Tyacke
1901-1903	R. Combe Miller D.L.
1901-1920	F. Baring Du Pre
1903-1911	Archibald Francis Fletcher Smith

With the implementation of the new Scheme in 1904 the position of the Trustees changed to that of Governor.

1904-1916	John W. Woods
1904-1924	Thomas Weller-Poley
1904-1932	George Ashley Tyacke
1904-1920	F. Baring Du Pre
1904-1910	Payton Temple Mackeson
1904-1911	A.F.F. Smith
1904-1914	William D. Jones
1910-1939	W. Lewis Gibbings
1913-1922	Admiral Swinton C. Holland
1914-1937	Arthur W. Henty
1916-1950	Sir William B.M. Bird

1920-1946	W. Seymour Eastwood
1922-1940	Capt. E.H. Weller-Poley
1924-1949	Adml. R.S. Phipps Hornby
1932-1947	Vice Adml. A.K. Macrorie
1937-1949	Adml. The Hon Sir Herbert Meade-Fetherstonhaugh
1939-1948	Vice Adml. G.T.C.P. Swabey
1944-1949	Eng. Vice Adml. Sir Reginald W. Skelton
1946-1949	Brig. O.L. Prior Palmer
1948-1949	Richard I. Henty

Appendix II

Headmasters

1712–1749	Robert Clarke	1810–1841	Henry Pescod
1749–1792	Israel Killwick	1841–1871	Thomas Pescod
1792–1797	James McDonald	1871–1908	Charles H.R. Ballard
1797–1808	Thomas Hackman	1908–1931	Charles Fairbrother
1808–1810	William Wheatley	1931–1949	Horace A. Spendlove

46 Two Old Boys (Ralph Lawrence and Maurice Page, *right*) standing beside the 'Roll of Honour—Best Scholar' board. The board is currently in the care of the Chichester and District Museum.

Appendix III

Roll of Honour—Best Scholar

1902	H. Lanscombe	1918	A.G. Bridle	1934	R. Law
1903	W.L. Norris	1919	H.R. Humphrey	1935	P. Milverton
1904	W.S. Rousell	1920	D.J. Weaver	1936	L.W. Bridger
1905	E.F. Humphrey	1921	J.F. Taylor	1937	J. Groundsell
1906	F.J. Chandler (W)	1922	F.J. Eade	1938	D. Dibley
1907	A.J.M. Green (H)	1923	V.E. Chaffer	1939	R.A. Stenning
1908	G. Ayling	1924	R. Arnold	1940	R. Shippam
1909	E.G. Brewer	1925	A.H.T. Daniels	1941	J.D. Yeo
1910	G.W.W. Latter	1926	J. Gale	1942	J.D. Yeo
1911	E.D. Patter (W)	1927	H.F. Cates	1943	D Randall
1912	F. Shippam	1928	N. Waddington	1944	F. Butler
1913	F.W.C. Ayling	1929	L.A. Taplin	1945	A. Carter (H)
1914	R.G. Edwards (H)	1930	J.W. Scutt	1946	A. Carter (H)
1915	L.J. Petter (W)	1931	A.W. Groundsell	1947	P. Hines (H)
1916	H.S. Haywood	1932	J. Greenfield	1948	R. Lawrence (W)
1917	T.J. Ayling	1933	H.E.R. Watson	1949	J. Messam

(H)   Harting Boys

(W)   West Wittering Boys

Remainder were Chichester Boys.

Appendix IV

Inscription on Playing Field—Memorial Stone

(As inscribed)

THIS PLAYING FIELD
WAS PURCHASED IN 1926 BY
THOMAS WELLER-POLEY AND HIS
SON CAPTAIN E H WELLER-POLEY
AND WAS PRESENTED BY THEM TO
OLIVER WHITBY SCHOOL, CHICHESTER
IN MEMORY OF THE LATE
THOMAS WELLER-POLEY ESQ, J.P.
OF WEST BROYLE WHO WAS A GOVERN
OR FOR 29 YEARS AND CHAIRMAN
FOR 21 YEARS, TOOK AN UNREM
ITTING INTEREST IN THE PROS
PERITY OF THE SCHOOL AND THE
HAPPINESS OF ITS SCHOLARS

(This Memorial Stone is still on its original site, at the south-west corner of the 12th Chichester Scout Headquarters, Sherborne Road, Chichester.)

Appendix V

Bathing Instructions—Easter Term, 1939

Each boy must adhere strictly to the following rules:

1 Go to the bathroom in slippers.
2 Be in possession of two towels.
3 Be ready to enter the bath at the time stated.

4 Quit the bath within twelve minutes and leave it clean.
5 Take care that all belongings are taken away.
6 Be out of the bathroom 10 minutes after leaving the bath.

Bath-time (p.m.)		Bathers			
4- 0	Supervisors:	Burnand I	&	Dibly	alternately
4-12		Messam		West I	
4-24		Cook		Gregory	
4-36		Strong		Shippam II	
4-48		Ashman		Billinghurst II	
5- 0		Burnand II		Groundsell	
5-12		Billinghurst I		Hornsby	
5-24	Supervisors:	Ede	&	Ayling	alternately
5-36		Page		Baker	
5-48		Randall		Morge	
6- 0		West II		Skilton	
6-12		Johnson		Tidy II	
6-24		Williams		Marsh	
6-36		Yeo		Moon	
6-48	Supervisors:	Shippam I	&	Stenning	alternately
7-0		Plumbridge		Hellyer	
7-12		Samways		George	
7-24		Finch		Butler	
7-36		Bowles		Edmonds	
7-48		Saxton		Tidy I	

The last boys must see the baths clean, the bathroom tidy, and be at supper by 8-20 p.m.

(Signed by Horace A. Spendlove)
Head Master.

Appendix VI

Letter given to Boys at the Closing of the School

VIS ET SAPIENTIA

THE OLIVER WHITBY SCHOOL,
CHICHESTER.

My dear

      You have had a great misfortune in having your association with us in study and living together cut short, but we want you to understand that we are still interested in you and shall keep contact with those responsible for your further education.

      If you have gained under our care the hall-mark of trustworthiness, reliability, good manners and manliness we shall be happy. Make up your mind that you will lose nothing of these qualities, but foster and strengthen them and decide that the break in your education is not going to be your loss.

      Take this gift,- a beautiful Bible- from the Governors and let it be your guide through life: it will never fail you, and whenever you are puzzled seek its advice. You cannot do better than live within Christ's precepts and make your friends of those who follow Him.

      Accept our best wishes for your future;- go from strength to strength.

      Yours very sincerely,

      Headmaster.

Copy of Programme of Plays performed by the Boys

1	Incidental Music		A. Carter
2	Play,	– 'Six Who Pass While The Lentils Boil.' By Stuart Walker.	

      Scene,   –   A Kitchen.
      Period,   –   When you will.
      Caste,   –   in order of appearance.

Prologue,	K. Morey
The Device-Bearer	R. Hill
You	E. Smith
The Boy	J. Messam
The Queen	D. Johnson
The Mime	M. Page
The Milkmaid	J. Haffenden
The Blindman	D. Aslett
The Ballard-Singer	L. Burnand
The Dreadful Headsman	P. Welch

3	Song,	– 'Bless This House'	Mrs. Spendlove
4	Play,	– 'The Doubtful Misfortune of Li Sing' By Neil Tuson	

      Scene,   –   The Living-room in the Farmhouse of Li Sing.
      Caste,   –   in order of appearance.

Li Sing, an impoverished farmer	A. Carter
His Wife, equally impoverished	P. Hines
Ling Fo, a creditor	M. Patey
Wong, another creditor	R. Yeo
a Third Creditor	R. Hill
Hung Hy, robber leader	R. Lawrence
First Robber	G. Marshall
Second Robber	J. Haffenden
Third Robber	R. Dorey

5	Songs,	– 'The Kingsway.' & 'When You Come Home.'	Mrs Spendlove
6	Play,	– 'Sunset at Baghdad' by F. Sladen-Smith.	

      Scene,   –   A Street in Baghdad.
      Caste,   –   in order of appearance.

The Blackamoor	P. Hines
The Prophet	A. Carter
The Hag	G. West
The Girl	R. Lawrence
The Prince	P. Hughes

7	Christmas Carol	The Boys
8	The National Anthem	

'Strength and Wisdom' by William James Barnes

There was a School
In my hometown,
Where Sunday dress
Was a long blue gown.
With a silver badge,
And a girdle of leather,
An apprentice's cap
For inclement weather.

Seventeen hundred and two
Was the year.
And Oliver Whitby
Had made it clear,
That twelve poor boys
Would have education,
With special attention
To navigation.

They came
From Chichester, Witt'ring and Harting,
When they heard
Of a special school that was starting,
For boys who had not heard the sound before,
Of 'Opportunity'
Knocking their door.

I went to that school,
Nineteen forty one.
Though my school days, for years
Have been over and done,
I still have the knowledge,
And that learning desire,
Due largely,
To Oliver Whitby Esquire.

Thank You!

Written by William James (Bill) Barnes (Old Boy 1941-1945), Canada 2001.

Special Choral Service to mark the Tercentenary of the Death of Oliver Whitby

THE CATHEDRAL CHURCH OF THE HOLY TRINITY, CHICHESTER

Tuesday, 19 February, 2002 at 4.00 pm.

ORDER OF SERVICE

The Choir will sing from the South Transept

Teach me, O Lord, the way of thy statutes,
and I shall keep it unto the end.

Words: Psalm 119   Music: Thomas Attwood (1765–1838)
A Fanfare

Please stand for the Processional Hymn

Immortal, invisible, God only wise,
In light inaccessible hid from our eyes,
Most blessed, most glorious, the Ancient of Days,
Almighty, victorious, thy great name we praise.

Unresting, unhasting, and silent as light,
Nor wanting, nor wasting, thou rulest in might;
Thy justice like mountains high soaring above
Thy clouds which are fountains of goodness and love.

To all life thou givest – to both great and small;
In all life thou livest, the true life of all;
We blossom and flourish as leaves on the tree,
And wither and perish – but nought changeth thee.

Great Father of glory, pure Father of light,
Thine angels adore thee, all veiling their sight;
All laud we would render: O help us to see
'Tis only the splendour of light hideth thee.

Introduction

Remain standing for the Opening Prayer during which a large candle will be lit representing the light of the Risen Christ—the source of all knowledge and the inspiration for all learning

> Blessed are you, O Lord our God, ruler of the universe!
> You led your people Israel by a pillar of cloud by day and a pillar of fire by night.
> Enlighten our darkness by the light of your Christ.
> May his word be a lamp, to our feet and a light to our path; for you are full
> of loving kindness for your whole creation, and we, your creatures, glorify
> you, Father, Son and Holy Spirit, now and for ever.   Amen.

The Priest will invite all present to call to mind their sins and failings. After a short pause, he will say:

> The word of God is living and active.
> It judges the thoughts and intentions of the heart.
> All is open and laid bare before the eyes of him to whom we give account.
> We confess our sins in penitence and faith.
>
> May your loving kindness come to me, O Lord and your salvation
> according to your word:
> Lord, have mercy.

All: Lord, have mercy.

> Your word is a lantern to my feet and a light to my path:
> Christ, have mercy.

All: Christ, have mercy.

> O let your mercy come to me that I may live, for your law is my delight:
> Lord, have mercy.

All: Christ, have mercy.

The Priest will pray a prayer for forgiveness

Please sit

The Choir shall sing Psalm 33

Rejoice in the Lord, O ye righteous: for it becometh well the just to be thankful.

Praise the Lord with harp: sing praises unto him with the lute, and instrument of ten strings.

Sing unto the Lord a new song: sing praises lustily unto him with a good courage.

For the word of the Lord is true: and all his works are faithful.

He loveth righteousness and judgement: the earth is full of the goodness of the Lord.

By the word of the Lord were the heavens made: and all the hosts of them by the breath of his mouth.

He gathereth the waters of the sea together, as it were upon an heap: and layeth up the deep, as in a treasure-house.

Let all the earth fear the Lord: stand in awe of him, all ye that dwell in the world.

For he spake, and it was done: he commanded, and it stood fast.

The Lord bringeth the counsel of the heathen to nought: and maketh the devices of the people to be of none effect, and casteth out the counsels of princes.

The counsel of the Lord shall endure for ever: and the thoughts of his heart fromgeneration to generation.

Blessed are the people, whose God is the Lord Jehovah: and blessed are the folk, that he hath chosen to him to be his inheritance.

The Lord looked down from heaven, and beheld all the children of men: from the habitation of his dwelling he considereth all them that dwell on the earth.

He fashioneth all the hearts of them: and understandeth all their works.

There is no king that can be saved by the multitude of an host: neither is any mighty man delivered by much strength.

A horse is counted but a vain thing to save a man: neither shall he deliver any man by his great strength.

Behold, the eye of the Lord is upon them that fear him: and upon them that put their trust in his mercy;

To deliver their soul from death: and to feed them in the time of dearth.

Our soul hath patiently tarried for the Lord: for he is our help and our shield.

For our heart shall rejoice in him: because we have hoped in his holy Name.

Let thy merciful kindness, O Lord, be upon us: like as we do put our trust in thee.

All stand while the Choir sing the Gloria

Glory be to the Father, and to the Son: and to the Holy Ghost:

As it was in the beginning, is now, and ever shall be: world without end. Amen.

Please sit

The First Reading
Proverbs, Chapter 8, Verses 11–12 and Verses 32–35
read by Jack Hutton-Potts, most recent Oliver Whitby Scholar at Christ's Hospital

Please stand for the Founder's Hymn

Our hearts and voices we would raise
In gratitude, O Lord, to thee.
Accept our artless song of praise,
And let us all Thy children be.

O may our future conduct show
Instruction has not been in vain;
Do Thou Thy saving grace bestow,
And make our path of duty plain.

Sweet charity, the bond of peace,
Inspired our Founder's noble soul.
O may the virtue still increase,
And all our acts and thoughts control.

The task Thy wisdom hath assigned,
O let us cheerfully fulfil,
In all our works Thy presence find,
And gladly do Thy Holy Will.

Hallelujah, Hallelujah, Hallelujah. Amen.

Please sit

A Tribute [see p. ix]
by Dr Geoffrey Barnard, former Communar of the Cathedral

The Choir shall sing the Anthem

Let all the world in every corner sing,
My God and King!
The heavens are not too high,
His praise may thither fly;
The earth is not too low,
His praises there may grow.
Let all the world in every corner sing,
My God and King!

Let all the world in every corner sing,
My God and King!
The Church with psalms must shout,
No door can keep them out;
But above all, the heart
Must bear the longest part.
Let all the world in every corner sing,
My God and King!

Words: George Herbert (1593-1633)   *Music: Ralph Vaughan Williams (1872-1958)*

The Second Reading
Ephesians, Chapter 3, Verses 14-21
read by Mr John McKerchar, Chairman of the Oliver Whitby Educational Foundation

Please sit

The Homily
The Reverend Canon Godfrey Hall
Head Master of the Prebendal School, former Assistant Chaplain and Housemaster at Christ's Hospital

Please stand for the Hymn

God moves in a mysterious way,
His wonders to perform;
He plants his footsteps in the sea,
And rides upon the storm.

Deep in unfathomable mines
Of never-failing skill
He treasures up his bright designs,
And works his sovereign will.

Ye fearful saints, fresh courage take,
The clouds ye so much dread
Are big with mercy, and shall break
In blessings on your head.

Judge not the Lord by feeble sense,
But trust him for his grace;
Behind a frowning providence
He hides a smiling face.

His purposes will ripen fast,
Unfolding every hour;
The bud may have a bitter taste,
But sweet will be the flower.

Blind unbelief is sure to err,
And scan his work in vain;
God is his own interpreter,
And he will make it plain.

Please kneel for the Prayers

Let us pray to the Lord, saying:

All: Lord, have mercy.

For the peace that comes from God alone, for the unity of all peoples, and for the salvation of our souls, let us pray to the Lord.
All: Lord, have mercy.

For the Church of Christ, for John our Bishop and for the whole people of God, let us pray to the Lord.
All: Lord, have mercy.

For the nations of the world, for Elizabeth our Queen and for all in authority, let us pray to the Lord.
All: Lord, have mercy.

For this city and for our neighbours and our friends, let us pray to the Lord.
All: Lord, have mercy.

For the good earth which God has given us, and for the wisdom and will to conserve it, let us pray to the Lord.
All: Lord, have mercy.

For the aged and infirm, for the widowed and orphans, for the sick and suffering and for all in any need, let us pray to the Lord.
All: Lord, have mercy.

For the poor and the oppressed, for the unemployed and the destitute, for prisoners and captives, and for all who remember and care for them, let us pray to the Lord.
All: Lord, have mercy.

For the dying, for those who mourn and for the faithful whom we entrust to the Lord in hope, as we look forward to the day when we share the fulness of the resurrection, let us pray to the Lord.
All: Lord, have mercy.

Rejoicing in the communion of all the saints, let us commend ourselves, and one another, and all our life, to God.

The Choir shall sing

> God be in my head, and in my understanding;
> God be in mine eyes, and in my looking;
> God be in my mouth, and in my speaking;
> God be in my heart, and in my thinking;
> God be at mine end, and at my departing.

Sarum Primer, 1558   *John Rutter (b.1945)*

Prayer of Thanksgiving for Oliver Whitby

We thank you, Lord, that in every age you not only raise up men as leaders within their generation, but also men with humbler ambitions who seek to do your will in their daily lives and in service to you and to others.

On this 300th anniversary, we remember with grateful thanks, Oliver Whitby who served as Precentor in a cathedral church similar to this for many years – who walked in the cloisters and within these walls as we walk here today; for his vision of service beyond his earthly life, by the setting up of a school for under-privileged boys and providing for their human needs and education. We thank you Lord, that you have called others over the years, who have also encompassed this vision, and offered their services to ensure this work has continued. The trustees and governors, the head masters and masters, whose devotion and service has ensured that several hundreds of boys' lives have been enriched. We thank you for their sacrifice, and that of their families, who have sustained them, often through difficult times.

We pray that through the power of your Holy Spirit, this work may continue in the years ahead, so through it your name may be glorified. We ask all this in the precious Name of Jesus. Amen.

Please stand

Fanfare *before the closing Hymn, during which a collection will be taken for the mission of the Cathedral*

> Lord of all hopefulness, Lord of all joy,
> Whose trust, ever child-like, no cares could destroy,
> Be there at our waking, and give us, we pray,
> Your bliss in our hearts, Lord, at the break of the day.
>
> Lord of all eagerness, Lord of all faith,
> Whose strong hands were skilled at the plane and the lathe,
> Be there at our labours, and give us, we pray,
> Your strength in our hearts, Lord, at the noon of the day.
>
> Lord of all kindliness, Lord of all grace,
> Your hands swift to welcome, your arms to embrace,
> Be there at our homing, and give us, we pray,
> Your love in our hearts, Lord, at the eve of the day.
>
> Lord of all gentleness, Lord of all calm,
> Whose voice is contentment, whose presence is balm,
> Be there at our sleeping, and give us, we pray,
> Your peace in our hearts, Lord, at the end of the day.

Please kneel

The Blessing

Select Bibliography

Most of the **Manuscript Authorities** used in preparing this book are gathered E35/A and E35/D, housed in the West Sussex Record Office. These include:

Trustees Account Books of which some include the Minutes of the Trustees, 1702-1898
Trustees Minute Books from 1833-1904
Extracts of Governors Minutes, 1904-1919
Admission Registers
Articles of the School and Inventory
Minutes and Records of the Lancastrian School, Chichester
Minutes and Records of the Central Schools, Chichester

In addition a number of **Original Record Sources** are from items housed in the Chichester Diocesan Record Office. These include:

Dean and Chapter of Chichester Act Books
Parish Registers of Chichester, West Wittering, Harting and Birdham
Grey Coat School Accounts
St. Mary's Hospital, Leases and Accounts

Other Original Record Sources
Principal Probate Registry
Public Record Office (Suits of Edes v Whitby)
British Museum (Miscellanea relating to Chichester and Sussex)
Archives of the City of Chichester (Minutes of the Common Council of the City of Chichester)
Headquarters of the S.P.C.K., London (Including Abstracts of Correspondence, Minutes and Circular Letters)
Census Returns, Chichester
Churchwardens Accounts, Harting, Sussex

Printed Materials
House of Lords journal and Calendar
House of Commons journal
Local papers (*Chichester Observer, West Sussex Gazette, Hampshire Telegraph and Sussex Daily News*)
Publications of the Sussex Archaeological Society
Publications of the Sussex Record Society
State Papers, Domestic
Reports of the Commission to Inquire Concerning Charities, 1819-1837
Reports of the Schools Inquiry Commission, 1866
Report of the Bryce Commission on Secondary Education
Education Acts of 1870, 1902, 1918

Index

Italic page numbers refer to illustrations; bold numbers refer to the Appendices

advertisements, for applicants, 36, 108
Allen, Francis, Trustee, **115**
Ansell, Joe, assistant master, 84
apprenticing system, 19–20, 41
Archer, John, sponsored at Christ's Hospital, 109
Ardingly College, 33
Arnold, R., best scholar, **117**
Aslett, Dennis, football team, 75
Ayling, F.W.C., best scholar, **117**
Ayling, G., best scholar, **117**
Ayling, Louise, cook, 85
Ayling, Marjorie, housemaid, 85
Ayling, T.J., best scholar, **117**
Aylmore, Councillor, 53

badge, 10–11, 20, 80, 88; worn by Oliver Whitby scholars at Christ's Hospital, xiii
Baker, Charles, Trustee, **115**
Baker, Christopher John, sponsored at Christ's Hospital, 109
Baker, Doug, Old Boy, xi
Baker, James, master of Central School, 26, 27
Ballard, C.H.R.: as assistant master, 34, 84; character, 37, 46, 89; on City Council, 57–8; illness and retirement, 63; as Master of School (1871-1908), 35, 35, 38–41, 45, 59, 80; recollections of, 82; salary, 42
Banks, Eric, Chichester Town Clerk, 102, 103, 109
Banks, Mr, assistant master, 84
Barcroft, William, 9
Baring Du Pre, F., Trustee, **115**
Barnard, Edward, Cathedral verger, 17
Barnard, Dr Geoffrey, tercentenary address, ix–xi

Barnes, William James, poem by, **122**
Baxton, John, Trustee, **115**
Bell, Dr Andrew, mutual system of education, 24, 27
Bell, George, Bishop of Chichester, 79–80, 106
Bennet, William, first Harting scholar, 14
Beveridge, David Anthony, 108
Beveridge, Mrs D.H., 108
Bevis, Michael G., Clerk to the Foundation Governors, 110
Bew, Mr, and Prior's scheme, 53, 54–5
Bird, Miss Valerie, Clerk to the Foundation Governors, 110
Bird, Sir William: Chairman of Governors, 69, 73, 81, 98, **115**; retirement, 109
Birdham: National School, 26; schoolhouse funded by Trust, 73
Bishop Luffa Church of England School, Chichester, 80
Bishop's Palace, Chichester, 21
Blackall, Rev. Lawrence, vicar of West Wittering, 107
Blomfield, Sir Reginald, architect of new school building, 59, 63, 113
Bloomfield, Mr, assistant master, 84
Blue Coat Girls School, Chichester, 24, 25, 26
Blue Coat Schools, xiii; Birmingham, 59; Liverpool, xiii, 35; see also Christ's Hospital
Board of Education Act (1899), 57
Boer War, 56, 58
Boots, John, at Grey Coat School, 15
Bostock, Dr Arthur: opposition to drainage schemes, 33, 50; and Prior's scheme, 54, 55
Bosworth, Mr, master of Lancastrian School, 26
Boy Scout troop, 6th Chichester, 68
Brereton, William, Trustee, 25, **115**

131

Brewer, E.G., best scholar, **117**
Brideoake, Ralph, Bishop of Chichester, 2
Bridger, L.W., best scholar, **117**
Bridger, Messrs, uniform supplier, 88
Bridle, Arthur G.: best scholar, **117**; Foundation
    Governor, 102, 109
Briggs, Thomas, 2
Brighton, annual outings to, 41, 93
Brisbane, Sir James, Trustee, **115**
Brougham, Henry Peter, M.P., 26–7
Browne-Wilkinson, Canon, Precentor, 77
Bryce, Mr, Commission on Secondary Educa-
    tion (1892), 51
Buckner, Richard, Trustee, **115**
Bull, Robert, Trustee, **115**
Bullicke, Anthony, of Harting, 1
Burdett, Robert P., Clerk to the Foundation
    Governors, 105, 111
Burnand, Bob, Old Boy, *xi*
Burnand, Eric: Old Boy, *xi*; football team, *75*
Burnand, Les, Old Boy, *xi*
Burnett, Mr, singing master, 22
Burrows, Mr, Board of Education inspector, 63
Butler, F., best scholar, **117**

Campbell Cook, B., County Librarian, 103
Carleton, Bishop, of Chichester, 3
Carr, Thomas, trustee, 5, 8, **115**
Carter, Alan: best scholar, **117**; Old Boy, *xi*
Cates, H.F., best scholar, **117**
Cathedral School *see* Prebendal School
central heating, 89
Central Schools, Chichester, xiii, 25–6, 27, 28, 35;
    employment for girls, 27, 28–9; finances, 31
Chaffer, V.E., best scholar, **117**
Chandler, F.J., best scholar, **117**
Chapel Street, bomb in, 71, *71*
Chappell, Katherine, witness to Whitby's will, 7
charity children, annual parades, 10, 22
Charity Commission, 38; Greenwood's inspec-
    tion (1884), 41–4; and Prior's scheme, 51, 52;
    and Snuggs's campaign, 44–5; Trust funds
    transferred to (1884), 44
Charity School movement, xiii, 10–12, 13, 23
charity schools, 8–9, 13, 25; administration of,
    16; funding, 10
charity sermons, 10, 21, 22, 27
Chichester: 18th-century rebuilding, 21; charity
    schools, 13, 51; drainage campaigns, 29–30,
    32–3, 45, 50; education in, 28, 48–9; inad-
    equacy of technical education, 52; late 19th-
century, 49–50; pupils from, 11, 20; second-
    ary education, 57, 60, 68; Whitby's bequest
    to poor, 7
Chichester Cathedral: boys' attendance at, 70,
    91–2; collapse of spire (1861), 31; Oliver
    Whitby window, *89*; Oliver Whitby's monu-
    ment in, 7, *89*; pew rent, 17, 22, 32; provi-
    sion for parish worship, 16; Tercentenary
    Service, **123–7**
Chichester Cathedral, Dean and Chapter: and
    decision to close School, 77–8, 79–80, 101;
    and new Scheme (1951), 106–7; opposition
    to Prior's scheme, 53–4, 55
Chichester City (Town) Council: and Coore's
    scheme, 59–60; and disposal of School
    property, 102, 103; finances, 22; and Prior's
    education scheme (1896–7), 51–6; representa-
    tive Foundation Governor, 110
Chichester Diocesan Education Committee,
    78–9, 101; Representative Foundation
    Governor, 110
Chichester Harbour, 20
Chichester High School for Boys (1928), 57,
    68, 73
Chichester Observer, 49; and Prior's scheme, 52,
    54
Chichester Theological College, 32
Chitty, Charles, 92
cholera, 28, 32
Christ's Hospital, Horsham, ix, 35, 43; annual
    parade, 10; co-education at, 112; and decision
    to close Oliver Whitby, 77, 101–2; fees, 106,
    111; Mathematical School, 9; memorabilia
    from Oliver Whitby School, 109; Oliver
    Whitby scholarships, x, xiii, 78, 101–2;
    selection and sponsorship procedure, 108–9
Church of England: and schools, 16, 28–9; and
    status of Oliver Whitby School, 79–80; *see
    also* Chichester Cathedral
cinema visits, 69, 93
Clarke, Robert: and Grey Coat School, 3, 15;
    master of Oliver Whitby School (1712–49),
    13, 17, 80; retirement and pension, 20
Clayton, Elizabeth, witness to Whitby's will, 7
cleanliness: Ballard's obsession with, 38, 82, 89;
    washrooms and baths, 89–90, **119**
Codrington, Rev. Robert Henry, vicar of West
    Wittering, 104
Collins, R.F., Old Boy, 53
Collins, William, Old Boy and poet, 114
'Colonel' (horse), *74*, 92

Commissioners on the Education of the Poor (1819): evidence from Trustees, 26–7; interpretation of Whitby's instructions, 7–8

Coombe Miller, R., Trustee, 61, **115**

Coore, G.B.M., Board of Education Commissioner, scheme for reforms (1904), 59–61

Costello, John, Trustee, **115**

Courtney, Ivan, 108

Courtney, Reg, in Sunday best, *76*

Cox, Mr, County Education officer, 73

Crimean War, 30

Crystal Palace, annual outing, 45

customs, 41, 97–8

Daniels, A.H.T., best scholar, **117**

Dartmouth Grammar School, 9

Davies, Captain Taff, Foundation Governor, 110

Davis, Evan, County Director of Education, 73

Dawes, George, Old Boy, 114

Dawson-Paul, Anthony, Foundation's stockbroker, 111

Dearling, Ted, Old Boy, *xi*

Dibley, Doug: best scholar, **117**; Old Boy, *xi*

Diggens, Francis, Trustee, **115**

discipline: under Ballard, 40, 95; under Fairbrother, 63, 68, 82, 95

Dissenters *see* Nonconformists

Dolphin Hotel, 30, 98

Doncaster, Richard, 108; football team, *75*

Dufton, Mr, Inspector of Science and Art Department, 52, 55

Duncan-Jones, A.S., Dean of Chichester, 77, 78, 80; closing service in Cathedral, *78*

Dunchurch endowed school, 10

Durnford, Bishop, of Chichester, 49, 51

Eade, F.J., best scholar, **117**

earthquakes (1734), 19

Eastwood, W. Seymour, Governor, **115**

Eddis, A.C., Charity Commissioner, 45; and Coore's reforms, 60; and Prior's scheme, 54, 55–6; recommendations (1891), 46–8

Edes, Dr Henry, 2; and Monmouth, 3, 4–5

education: mutual (monitorial) system, 24–5, 27; national inspection scheme, 32; state grants for, 24; state provision, 27, 45–6, 58; *see also* secondary education; voluntary system

Education Act: (1870), xiii, 34, 35; (1880), 45; (1891), 46; (1902), 46; (1944), 73

Edwards, R.G., best scholar, **117**

Eggar, Thomas, 106

electric light, 68

elementary schools: compulsory attendance, 45; reforms, 24–5

Elleker, Michael, football team, *75*

Ellis, L.B., 11

endowed schools, 10, 38

Endowed Schools Commission, 38

escapades, 94–5

Evans, E.T., representative Foundation Governor, 110

Evans, R.C., Clerk of Christ's Hospital, 77, 101–2, 108

Fairbrother, Charles, Master of School (1908-31), 63, 68, 80, 82

Fairbrother, Mrs, *67*, 83

Fairbrother Memorial Prize, 98

Farhill, George, Trustee, **115**

Farrington, Richard, 4

First World War, 68

Flecker, H.L.O., Headmaster of Christ's Hospital, 108

Fletcher, Mr, assistant master, 37

Fletcher, Peter, Old Boy, *xi*

Florance, James, City Surveyor, 26

Floyd, Arthur, Foundation Governor, 104, 105, 110

Forebench, Jane, 'servant' of School, 19

Forebench, Thomas, 19

Founder's Day, 97–8

Freeland, Mr, and drainage campaign, 32–3

Gale, J., best scholar, **117**

Gardener, Thomas, apprenticed, 23

Garland, Alderman, 55

Gibbings, W. Lewis, Governor, **115**

Giffard, H.A., Commissioner (1867), 33–4

Gilbert, Arthur, sponsored by Foundation, 109

Goater, Francis: executor of Whitby's will, 7, 8; as Treasurer of Trustees, 13, 18, 20, **115**

Godding, Peter, of Harting, 1

Gounter, George, 8, **115**

Green, A.J.M., best scholar, **117**

Green, Mr, Master of Lancastrian School, 26

Green, Mr, assistant master, 37

Greenfield, J., best scholar, **117**

Grey Coat School, Chichester, 13, 15, 21, 24, 26; finances, 21, 23, 25

Grey Coat School, Westminster, 9, 35, 43

Grey of Werke, Ford, Lord, 3, 5

Groome, Douglas, Old Boy, 114

Groundsell, A.W., best scholar, **117**
Groundsell, J., best scholar, **117**
Gruggen, Thomas, at Grey Coat School, 15
Gunning, Peter, Bishop of Chichester, 2
gymnasium (1938), 69, *71*, 86, *86*; sale of, 103

Habin, Richard, 4
Hackman, Mr, Master of School (1797-1808), 23, 24
Haffenden, John, xi, 77, *94*; football team, *75*
Hall, Margaret, beneficiary of Whitby's will, 7
Halsted, Edith Emily, 111
Halsted, Roger Guy, bequest, 111
Hammett, Mrs Sara, JP, Foundation Governor, 110
Hammond, John, glazier, 17
Hampshire Telegraph, 27, 28, 29, 49
Hanbury, Nigel, Foundation Governor, 110
Hanbury, Peter, Foundation Governor, 105, 110, 111
Hanmore, Charles, 33
Harris, George, Trustee, **115**
Harris, J.D., assistant master, 84
Harris, Rev. Robert D., as representative Foundation Governor, 110
Harting: bequest to poor, 7; Oliver Whitby in, 1, 3; pupils from, 11, 14, 42, 106–7
Harvey, Mr, assistant master, 37
Hasler, Richard, Trustee, **115**
Hasler, William, Trustee, **115**
Hatcher, Michael, football team, *75*
Hayley, William, Dean of Chichester, xiii, 9
Haywood, H.S., best scholar, **117**
health, provision for, 17–18
Heath, Wilfred, 113
Henty, Arthur W., Governor, **115**
Henty, Colonel Richard, Governor; 73, 92, 106, 109, **115**; and proposal to close School, 77–8
Her Majesty's Inspectors of Schools, 32, 91
Herniman, C.D., as representative Foundation Governor, 110
Hill, John, first Harting scholar, 14
Hill, Robin, football team, *75*
Hines, P., best scholar, **117**
Hobbs, Archdeacon Keith, as representative Foundation Governor, 110
Hobbs, Mary, 110
Holdsworth, E.M., County Education Secretary, 105
Holland, Admiral Swinton, Governor, **115**
Hollingsworth, Mary, 'housewife' at School, 16, 18, 19

Holroyd, Mrs E.M., 104
Holt, Anne, 7
Holt, Thomas, executor of Whitby's will, 7, 8, **115**
Hoskins, John (Jack) and Frederick, in Sunday best, *76*
housekeepers, 16, 19, 20, 83–4; *see also* servants
Hughes, G.R., Ministry of Education, 106–7, 108
Hughes, Peter, Old Boy, xi
Hume, Joseph, 24
Humphrey, E.F., best scholar, **117**
Humphrey, H.R., best scholar, **117**
hymn, school, 10, 22–3

Ide, Bob, Old Boy, xi, 77
Ingram, Mr, master of Grey Coat School, 22
inoculation (against smallpox), 20, 84
inspections: Board of Education (1908), 63; by Commissioners (1819), 28; by Dr Morris, 37; Greenwood's (1884), 41–4
insurance, 19; life assurance policies, 105–6
Isle of Wight, camping holidays, 69, 93

Jamieson, P.W., legacy, 105
Jellett, Bob, Old Boy, xi
Jennings, William, Mayor of Chichester, 3
Johnson, John J., Trustee, 38, **115**
Johnson, William, Trustee, **115**
Jones, William D., Governor, **115**

Keys, F.R.S., Old Whitbyians Association, 101
Killwick, Israel: as master of Grey Coat School, 22; Master of School (1749-92), 20, 21
Kilmersdown endowed school, 10
King, Henry, Bishop of Chichester, ix, 2
Kingston-upon-Hull, residential charity school, 11
Knight, G., memorial cleaning, 89
Knight, R.H., Foundation Governor, 110, 111

Lake, John, Bishop of Chichester, 3
Lancaster, Joseph, monitorial system of education, 24–5, 27
Lancastrian School, Chichester, xiii, 25, 27, 28, 31, 35, 49
Langley, Peter, football team, *75*
Lanscombe, H., best scholar, **117**
Latter, G.W.W., best scholar, **117**
laundry, responsibility for, 37, 90
Law, R., best scholar, **117**

Lawrence, Ralph: best scholar, **117**; Old Boy, *xi*, 89, *116*
Lee, Joseph, bookseller, 17
Ling, H.J., Foundation Governor, 109
Linton, Miss, matron, 45
Lintott, Stephen, apprenticeship, 20
Local Government Act (1888), 46
Lowther-Clarke, Canon W.K., 77
Lucas, Samuel, pupil (died of smallpox), 18
Ludgate, Thomas, Trustee, **115**
Luton endowed school, 10

MacCahearty, David John, Clerk to the Foundation Governors, 111
McDonald, James, Master of School (1792-97), 22, 23
McKay, Mr, assistant master, 84
McKerchar, John, Foundation Governor, 110
Mackeson, Payton Temple, Governor, **115**
Macrorie, Vice Admiral A.K., Governor, **115**
Manning, Archdeacon, 28, 29
Manningham, Thomas, Treasurer of Chichester Cathedral, xiii, 9
Mant, Mr, assistant master, 84
Marsh, Mrs E., William and Peter, 77
Marshall, Mr, Headmaster of Brighton Grammar School, 55
Mason, Lancelot, Archdeacon, 77, 101, 106; as representative Foundation Governor, 110
'mathematical' schools, 9
May, Henry, Trustee, **115**
Meade-Fetherstonhaugh, Admiral the Hon. Sir H., Foundation Governor, 110, **115**
meals and diet, 40–1, 85, 95–6, 97
Mechanics Institute, 31
Menville, Thomas, pupil (died of smallpox), 20
Meredith, Rev. W.M., 54
Messam, John: best scholar, **117**; football team, *75*
Middle School, Chichester, 33
Middlesex Volunteers, 58
Middleton, Rev. Guy, Diocesan Educational Department, 106
'Midnight Walks', 94
Mill, John Stuart, 33
Miller, Sir John, M.P. and Trustee, 10, **115**
Milton, Walter, Trustee, **115**
Milverton, P., best scholar, **117**
Ministry of Education: and decision to close School, 73, 75, 78–80; and new Scheme (1951), 101, 106, 107–8
Mitten, Francis, clock maker, 17

Moffat, Dr, Board of Education inspector, 63
Monmouth, James, Duke of, 3, 4–5
Morants Ltd, 103, 113
Morgan, Mr, assistant master, 84
motto (*Vis et Sapientia*), 80
Murray, Sir John, Trustee, **115**
music and singing, 22, 91–2

National Schools, 26, 34
navigation, teaching of, 9, 23
Neale's Mathematical School, Fetter Lane, 9
Newcastle Commission, on education in England (1861), 32
Newland, Richard, Trustee, **115**
Newland, William, Trustee, **115**
night school, Chichester (1870), 30–1
Nonconformists, 28; and Coore's scheme, 60; and Prior's scheme, 52–3; Whitby's dislike of, 10
Norris, W.L., best scholar, **117**
Norwich Girls' Hospital school, 43

Old Boys: future lives, of 113, 114; reminiscences, 81–98, **99–100**
Old Oliver Whitbyians Association, 98–9, *98*, 109
Oliver Whitby Educational Foundation (1951), 101; investment of proceeds of sale, 103, 105; life assurance policies, 105–6; P.W. Jamieson Fund, 105; reinvestment of funds, 111; representative governors, 106–7; revised selection criteria, 107–8; scholarships to Christ's Hospital, x, xiii, 78, 101–2
Oliver Whitby Foundation: Account Book, 17; additional Trustees proposed, 43, 47, 48, 52; City Council representative, 59–60; County representative, 59; decision on future use of funds (from 1949), 79, 101; Eddis's recommendations (1891), 46–8; evidence to Commissioners (1819), 26–7; finances, 18, 21, 23, 26, 45; and funding for new buildings, 59, 60; and Greenwood's inspection (1884), 41–2, 43–4; insularity of Trustees, 36, 38, 43–4, 47–8, 57; new Scheme (1951), 101; and Pescod's pension, 36; rising expenditure, 58; school at West Wittering, 29; Snuggs's campaign against, 44–5; Trustees and Governors, **115**; *see also* Oliver Whitby Educational Foundation (1951)
Oliver Whitby School, x, xiii–xiv, 9–10, 11; academic status, 32, 37–8, 68, 69; Articles (rules), 15; assistant masters, 27, 37, 68, 69, 84;

boys' duties, 88–9; Charity Service (from 1779), 22; closing ceremonies, 78, 79, 102; Coore's reforms, 59–61; curriculum, 23, 30, 34, 39, 58, 59, 90–1; curriculum enlarged (1930s), 69; decision to close, 73, 75, 77–80; dining hall, 64, 96–7, 96; disposal of properties, 102–5, 113–14; first inventory, 14; garden, 29, 97; gifts from Trustees and Governors, 31, 81–2; Greenwood's recommendations, 42–3; independence of, 28, 61, 80; interiors, 64–5, 90; new buildings, 59, 60, 62, 85–7, 85; numbers of pupils, 8, 27, 34, 37, 45, 87; organ, xi; original building, 12, 13–14, 18, 27, 38, 43, 85; preparations for opening, 13–14; Prior's scheme, 51–6; proposed admission of day boys, 38, 43, 47–8, 52; public access to, 16–17, 91; reputation of, 42–3, 48–9; rising expenses, 68, 73, 75; Roll of Honour, 98, 116, 117; secondary education at, 60, 68; selection procedures, 14, 20, 36, 42; staircase, 90, 113–14; suggested annexation to Prebendal, 34, 38; suggested merger with Prebendal, 77–8; and Taunton Commission (1867), 33–4; teaching of mathematics (navigation), 6, 9, 23, 43, 90; timetable, 30, 38–41, 71, 88–9; under Ballard, 36–7, 38–41, 45; under Fairbrother, 63, 68; visits and exeats, 90, 94, 95; window bars, 17, 60, 85; see also Tower Street
outings, 28, 31, 93; annual, 41, 45, 74, 93; cinema, 69, 93; educational, 93; scout camps, 66–7; summer camps, 69, 72, 93; Sunday afternoon walks, 93
Owton, Richard, pupil, 18
Oxford Movement, 28
Oxford, Trinity College, 1

Page, Maurice, Old Boy, xi, 116
Page, Mr, County Education officer, 73
Pakeman, Miss, Matron, 83
Pallant House, Chichester, 20
Parke, John, Trustee, 115
Parker, Mr, of London, supplier of uniform, 15, 87
Parliament: grant to state education (1833), 24; Select Committee on the Education of the Lower Orders (1816), 26–7
Parnell, John, blacksmith, 23
Parnell, Joseph, apprenticed, 23
Parsons, J., examiner, 48
Patter, E.D., best scholar, 117
Paull, Mr, master of Lancastrian School, 26
Paull, Mr (junior), 27

Peachey, John, 5
Peachey, John, Trustee, 25, 115
Pearcey, Thomas, first Harting scholar, 14
Peckham, Henry 'Lisbon', 20
Peckham, Henry 'Mercer', 20, 21, 115
pensions, for retired Masters, 20, 36, 102
Pepys, Samuel, ix, 9
Pescod, Henry, Master of School (1810-41), 24, 26, 84
Pescod, Thomas, Master of School (1841-71), 31, 34, 84; illness and retirement, 35–6, 82
Petter, L.J., best scholar, 117
Petter, Mr, assistant master, 84
Petworth, ix, 2
Philmore, A.M., 94
Phipps Hornby, Admiral, 79, 80, 81–2; Foundation Governor, 109, 115; negotiations with Christ's Hospital, 101–2
Pierrepoint, John, 10
Piggott, James, Trustee, 115
Pilkington, Captain, 31
Pilkington, Edward W., Trustee, 115
Pink, Anthony, 20
playground, 70, 86
playing fields, 82, 92, 102, 118
plays, performances of, 98, 121
Pound, Mr, assistant master, 84
Powell, Canon A., 77
Prebendal School, Chichester, 1, 28, 29, 38, 49; Foundation loan to buy Rapers' building, 112; Foundation sponsorships for, 111; opposition to Coore's scheme, 61; suggested annexation of Oliver Whitby's, 34, 38; suggestion of merger, 77–8
Prior, Ebenezer, 60, 61; education scheme, 51–6; sanitation campaign, 49–50
Prior-Palmer, Brigadier O.L., Foundation Governor, 109, 115
prize-giving, 87, 98
Pryer, Mr, Old Boy, 99
public inspection: of Lancastrian school, 25; of Oliver Whitby School, 16–17
Pullinger, Mr, workhouse Relieving Officer, 49
Purchas, George, at Grey Coat School, 15
Racton, 8
Radley College, 33
Randall, D., best scholar, 117
Rankin, Rev. John, representative Foundation Governor, 110
Raper & Co., Solicitors, 110, 112
Rasell, Alfred, wire worker, 17

Red Maids School, Bristol, 8
Rees-Reynolds, K.C., purchase of school buildings, 103
Reform Bill celebrations, 28
Richmond and Gordon, Duke of, 21
Richmond, Mr, Charity Commissioner, 52
Robinson, Mr, editor of *West Sussex Gazette*, 56
Rogers, Dennis, Old Boy, *xi*
Rousell, W.S., best scholar, **117**
Royal Navy, ix, 9
Russell Purchase, G.A., representative Foundation Governor, 110
Rutterley, George, witness to Whitby's will, 7

St Andrew's Church, Chichester, 31
St Mary's Hospital, Chichester, 2, 4, 30
St Peter the Great church, West Street, 16, 30, 91
Salisbury, Francis, vicar of Harting, 7
Sancroft, William, Archbishop of Canterbury, 3
Scatliff, Simon, 17
School of Art, Chichester, 31
school boards, 45–6
Schools Inquiry Commission, 47
scout camps, *66–7*
Scutt, J.W., best scholar, **117**
Second World War, 69, 71, 73, 83–4, 97
secondary education: Chichester, 57, 60, 68; national provision of, 33, 45–6; at Oliver Whitby School, 60, 68; Royal Commission on (1892), 51
Selsey Lifeboat, 31
servants and underservants, 84–5; *see also* housekeepers
Shaxson, Major Eric Stanley, 73
Sherer, Mr, 20
Shiers, Mr, groundsman, 92
Shinfield endowed school, 10
Shippam, Alf, Old Boy, *xi*
Shippam, F., best scholar, **117**
Shippam, Mr, and Prior's scheme, 53
Shippam, R., best scholar, **117**
Shrubb, Florence Fanny, 104, 109
Sir John Williamson's Mathematical School, Rochester, 9
Skelton, Admiral Sir R.W., Foundation Governor, 109, **115**
smallpox, 17, 18, 20
Smith, Archibald Francis Fletcher, Trustee and Governor, **115**
Smith, Sir Archibald Levin, Trustee, **115**

Smith, Francis, Trustee, **115**
Smith, Mr: Chairman of Trustees (1897), 57; senior Trustee (1891), 48
Smith, Robert, witness to Whitby's will, 7
Smith, Thomas, apprenticed, 23
Smith, Thomas, Trustee, 2, **115**
Snailham, Harry, assistant master, 84
Snuggs, Charles, campaign against, 44–5
Society for the Education of the Poor of Chichester, 25
Society for Promoting Christian Knowledge, xiii, 8–9, 10; rules for charity schools, 16, 19
Soote, J.R.S., 109
Soote, Rosemary Ruth, 109
Spawton, Clifford, Foundation Governor, 110
Spencer, Arthur David, 108
Spendlove, Mrs Florence, Matron, 20, *69*, 83–4
Spendlove, Freda, ix, 84
Spendlove, Horace A., Headmaster (1931-49), 69, *69*, 70, 73, 75, 80; at first annual reunion, 98; funeral, 110; letter to boys, **120**; pension for, 102, 106; reminiscences of, 82–3, 92
Spendlove, Hugh, ix, 84
Spendlove, Roy, ix, 84
Spens Report on Secondary Education (1895), 51
Spershott, William, memoirs, 17
sports and games, *65*, *75*, 92–3; playing fields, 82, 92, 102, **118**
statue of Blue Coat Boy, 18–19, *19*, 109
Steale, Thomas, Trustee, **115**
Steel, Henry, 18
Stenning, R.A., best scholar, **117**
Stepney, George, Trustee, **115**
Stint, Mary, 'housewife' of School, 19
Storrs, Joshua, supplier of badges, 88
Stride, Walter, Governor of School, 73; and proposal to close School, 77–8, 101
Stuart, James, memorial cleaning, 89
summer camps, 69, *72*, 93
Sunday School movement, 23
Sussex Central Schools, 25
Sussex Daily News, and Prior's scheme, 52, 56
Sussex Society for the Education of the Infant Poor, 25
Swabey, Vice Admiral G.T.C.P., Governor, **115**
Swain, Mr, Board of Education inspector, 63
Symonds, H.W. (Jack), Clerk to the Governors, 73, 78, 101, 103; Foundation Governor, 110; and sale of assets, 103–4
Taplin, L.A., best scholar, **117**

Taunton Commission, on secondary education (1864), 33
Taunton, Richard, Trustee, **115**
Taylor, J.F., best scholar, **117**
Technical Institute, Chichester, 58
Technical Instruction Act (1889), 46
Tercentenary address, ix–xi
Tercentenary Service, **123**–7
Terry, James, servant, 7
Tower Street, No. 52 (cottage), 29, 86, 102
travel expenses, 108
Trodd, Stewart, Old Boy, *xi*, 99
Tuffnell, Rev., vicar of St Bartholomew's, 26
Tupper, Mr, master of Grey Coat School, 21, 22
Tutte, Randolph, 13
Tyacke, Dr, and drainage campaign, 32–3
Tyacke, George Ashley, Trustee and Governor, **115**
Tyacke, Nicholas, Trustee, **115**
Tyler, Brian, City Architect, 103
typhoid, 37

uniform, 10, *36*, 42–3, *76*, 87–8, *87*; battle-dress blouse, 77, 88; blazer, tie and pullover, 77, 88; studded shoes, 90
Uppark, 3

VE Day celebrations, 71, 81
Vick, Mr, builder, 63, 85
Vick, Mrs, Matron, 83, 95
Vickers, T.H., HM Inspector of Schools, 85
voluntary system of elementary education, 24–5, 46

Waddington, N., best scholar, **117**
Wakeford, John: Chapter Clerk, 18; Trustee, 19, **115**
Walsh, Canon, 77
water supply, 37, 85
Watson, H.E.R., best scholar, **117**
Watts, John, Trustee, **115**
Watts, Mr, carved Blue Coat Boy statue, 18
Weaver, D.J., best scholar, **117**
Weaver, F.W., 98
Welch, Peter, Old Boy, *75*, *94*
Weller, Ernest, Old Boy, *xi*
Weller-Poley, E.H., Governor, 82, 93–4, 102, **115**

Weller-Poley, Mrs, 80, 94
Weller-Poley, Thomas, Trustee and Governor, 82, 92, **115**
West Broyle, outings to, *74*, 93–4
West, Jack, Old Boy, *xi*
West Sussex County Council, 52, 59; Board of Education, 59–60; and Foundation's West Wittering properties, 104–5; representative Foundation Governor, 110
West Sussex Gazette, 29, 30–1, 32, 49; support for Prior's scheme, 53, 55–6
West Wittering: bequests to poor, 7, 8; Common Farm (Charity Farm), 18; and Coore's scheme, 61; lands at, 7–8, 13, 21, 41, 44, 103–5; lease of prebend of, 42; pupils from, 11, 20, 42, 107–8; school (financed by Oliver Whitby Trust), 29, *29*, 105; schoolmaster's house, 104–5; and Snuggs's campaign against Trustees, 44
Wheatley, Mr, Master of School (1808-10), 24, 82
Whitby, Ann, mother of founder, 1, 3, 4
Whitby, Anne, 7
Whitby, Dr Daniel, 2, 7
Whitby, Oliver, Archdeacon, ix, 1–2
Whitby, Oliver, Founder, ix, 1; arms of, 11; life and times, 1–5; monument in Chichester Cathedral, 7, *89*; portrait of, *frontispiece*, 97; Tercentenary address, ix–xi; Tercentenary Service, **123**–7; will, *6*, 7–8, 9–10
White, Gilbert, of Selborne, 10
Whitehead & Whitehead, estate agents, 102
Widdows, John, solicitor and Foundation Governor, 104, 109–10
Williams, Sir Hutchins, Trustee, **115**
Williams, John, Bishop of Chichester, xiii, 9
Williams, Peckham, Trustee, **115**
Winchester College, 1
Wood, Thomas, first Harting scholar, 14
Woodard Schools, 77
Woods, John, Trustee, 25, **115**
Woods, John W., Trustee and Governor, **115**
Woods, William L., Trustee, **115**

Yeo, J.D., best scholar, **117**
Young, Sir George, 54
Young, Mr, Secretary for Technical Education, 55